I0059348

LEADING
ENTREPRENEURS

AND

HOW THEY SUCCEED

LEADING ENTREPRENEURS

AND

HOW THEY SUCCEED

World Scientific

NEW JERSEY · LONDON · SINGAPORE · BEIJING · SHANGHAI · HONG KONG · TAIPEI · CHENNAI · TOKYO

Published by

World Scientific Publishing Co. Pte. Ltd.
5 Toh Tuck Link, Singapore 596224
USA office: 27 Warren Street, Suite 401-402, Hackensack, NJ 07601
UK office: 57 Shelton Street, Covent Garden, London WC2H 9HE

National Library Board, Singapore Cataloguing-in-Publication Data

Names: Enterprise 50 Association. | World Scientific Publishing Co., publisher.
Title: Leading Entrepreneurs and How They Succeed / E50 Association.
Description: Singapore : World Scientific Publishing Co. Pte. Ltd., [2016]
Identifiers: OCN 936133521 | ISBN 978-981-4759-93-9 (paperback) |
ISBN 978-981-31-4056-1 (hardcover)
Subjects: LCSH: Entrepreneurship—Singapore . | Small business—
Singapore—Management. | Businesspeople—Singapore.
Classification: LCC HB615 | DDC 658.421095957--dc23

British Library Cataloguing-in-Publication Data
A catalogue record for this book is available from the British Library.

Leading Entrepreneurs and How They Succeed

ISBN: 978-981-3140-56-1
ISBN: 978-981-4759-93-9(pbk)

Photographs by Yew Jia Jun (SidexSide Pictures)
https://www.facebook.com/sidexsidepictures/

Layout and design by Jimmy Low
In-house editor: Amanda Yun

Foreword

This book celebrates local entrepreneurs who have overcome adversities, found innovative ways to grow, and transformed their businesses over time. They have done so in diverse sectors and niches, but with each contributing in their own ways to Singapore's economic advancement.

There is much challenge ahead for Singapore businesses, given both the uncertainties of the global environment and the slowdown in growth of our labour force. However, there is also much opportunity, in Asia and elsewhere, even amidst the risks. Technology too will be a major enabler. It is bringing down the barriers for small businesses to scale up and compete globally.

These developments provide the context to the new phase of development that we have embarked on, one that is focused on creating value through innovation. It will require new capabilities, building on what our businesses and workforce has developed over the years. But it is these new innovative strengths and skills that will enable us to make the most of the opportunities of the future, and weather the problems that come our way.

We can achieve this transformation in our business sector and society, by drawing on the passions and strengths of every Singaporean, and helping everyone to keep learning through life.

The stories in this book give us confidence that we can do so. My congratulations to each of the entrepreneurs featured, and to the people who worked with them, for the inspiring journeys they have taken.

Tharman Shanmugaratnam
Deputy Prime Minister & Coordinating Minister for Economic and Social Policies

Contents

Introduction

Enterprise 50 Association (E50) was founded in 1999 with the mission to promote social interaction and a spirit of unity amongst E50 companies and entrepreneurs. In 1995, E50 established The Enterprise 50 Awards recognising local, privately-owned companies who have contributed to the economic development of Singapore and abroad. It has become a definitive list of the 50 most enterprising, privately-held local companies in Singapore.

E50 — 50for50 Book Project

With the vision of educating and inspiring the next generation of business leaders, E50 Management Committee are pleased to have engaged with local youth initiative, The Social Co. to document the stories and experiences of several entrepreneurs who will step forward to shape Singapore's economic future over the next 50 years. In your hand is a book that focuses not just on experience and knowledge, but also important human values such as compassion and love. It is also a timely project in the context of the SG50 celebrations held in 2015 to mark Singapore's 50th year as an independent nation.

Through this project, we managed to raise a total of $1.38million. These generous contributions donated by each company featured in this book have gone into supporting 25 charities. What better way is there, than to learn from and be inspired by those who have built business empires, forged new frontiers in their respective industries and yet consistently given back to society? We are proud of their contributions and these are the beneficiaries:

365 Cancer Prevention Society
aLife Limited
Alzheimer's Disease Association
APEX Day Rehabilitation for Elderly
Autism Association Singapore

Beyond Social Services
Bizlink
Casa Raudha Women Home
Children's Aid Society
Dyslexia Association of Singapore
Friends of the Disabled Society
Home Nursing Foundation
Hospice Care Association
Make-A-Wish Foundation
Malay Youth Literary Association
Movement for the Intellectually Disabled of Singapore
O'Joy Care Services
Sian Chay Medical Institution
Sree Narayana Mission (Singapore)
Student Advisory Centre
Thye Hua Kwan Moral Society
Singapore Association for Mental Health
Singapore Cancer Society
Singapore Children's Society
Very Special Arts and Viriya Community Services

I hope that you will find this book as meaningful and inspiring as I did, and I am looking forward to seeing E50 grow to greater heights.

Thank you.

Andy Lim
President, Enterprise 50 Association
Embracing Innovation, Empowering Enterprises, Emboldening Minds

*"Focus on your customers.
Have sufficient customers,
and hence income."*

Company Profile

AllAlloy is a total welding solutions provider, supplying high-end welding products (filler metals, welding machines, accessories and other consumables) to marine, oil and gas fabricators, offshore pipe-laying constructors as well as power plant and petrochemical constructors. Apart from supplying welding products, we also provide consultancy services and solutions to help enhance their customers' productivity.

Although a relatively young company, we have been serving the welding industry for more than 20 years. Progress has been rapid and the company has swiftly expanded abroad in the seven years since its incorporation, opening regional offices in Malaysia, Indonesia and Australia to meet the demands of overseas clientele.

Future plans include further geographical diversification and deeper market penetration with the aim of growing into a serious regional player. The next target markets are Vietnam, China and Myanmar. Innovation is also a vital cog and AllAlloy plans to introduce more products incorporating breakthrough technologies to help improve customer productivity. Efforts are also being made to bring in more cutting-edge products to enhance the product portfolio and to penetrate new markets.

Advice to Budding Entrepreneurs

- Do not jump into the market too hastily. It is vital to be thorough in one's research and equip yourself with sufficient knowledge before entering a market.
- For a new company, the various government grants available in Singapore can be an important lifeline to get past the teething stage.
- Always remember to keep an eye on your cash flow!
- Focus on your customers. Having sufficient customers, and hence income, to keep the business going is crucial. Be it courting new customers or building deeper relationships with existing customers, they are the lifeline of a business. Do not assume or think you have, always ENSURE you have sufficient customers to sustain the business.

Must-have Qualities of Successful Entrepreneurs

- Resilience and Will: to weather hardships and setbacks, and to pursue your goal no matter what obstacles stand in your way. And most importantly, be smart enough to go around the obstacles and not hit them straight on.
- Vision: to dare to dream big, and be able to guide the business where you want it to go.

- Contacts: to have people who can and are willing to lend a helping hand for the times when you need help most.

Turning Point

Being a young company of less than 10 years, there hasn't been any huge turning point for us yet. But clinching exclusive dealerships from major international players such as Air Liquide Welding (France), Sandvik (Sweden) as well as landing orders from big players in the oil and gas industry (Keppel, McDermott, Sembcorp Marine) were crucial in propelling the business forward, paving the way for us to win more orders with other international customers.

Significant Milestones

- Being awarded sole distribution rights from major international partners.
- Receiving financing from banks (DBS, Maybank, OCBC): financing was of paramount importance to AllAlloy when we first started out. And being able to obtain credit lines despite being a new startup really helped in getting our business going.
- Being awarded our first contracts from various big oil and gas fabricators, giving us a big boost in establishing our fledgling company in the industry.

The Next 50 Years

- More overseas-oriented
- Hopefully more of a global brand

Major Contributions to the Economy

We are just a young SME so I do not think our company has had any significant contribution to Singapore's economy yet, other than exporting our products overseas and paying taxes.

Global Footprint

AllAlloy is currently actively marketing two in-house brands: Revolloy (filler metal) and Revolt (welding automation and accessories) which we hope will become global brands eventually.

Name a Local Dish that Best Represents You or Your Business

Popiah. It represents a mixture of seemingly simple ingredients which somehow blend together to create a palate-satisfying dish.

Also, while every ingredient is important in creating the dish. No single ingredient stands out on its own, embodying one of our company's values of team spirit over individual effort.

And unlike another dish, the rojak, popiah has a structured exterior, thereby retaining a neat and composed feel amidst the chaos of ingredients.

Giving Back

Social responsibility is one of the key focuses of AllAlloy.

We firmly believe that no amount of effort is too small. As such, since our inception in 2008, the company has been supporting charity organisations from various social causes through corporate donations, sponsorships and staff participation in charity carnivals and runs, among other forms of support.

Staff are highly encouraged to take part in charity events the company participates in, as well as encouraged to propose new charitable initiatives of interest to them.

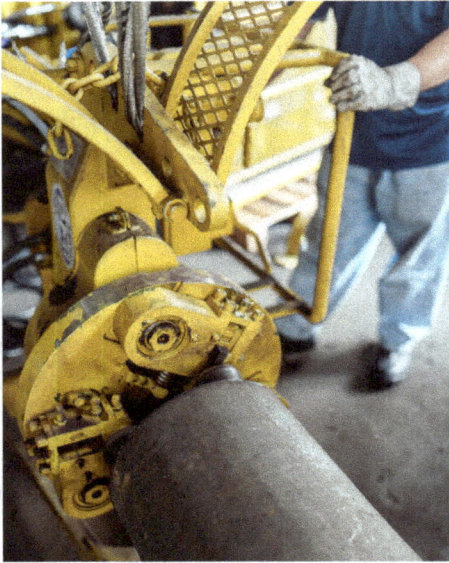

One company initiative started in 2011 to garner more support for local charities was to invite AllAlloy's customers and partners to participate in a movie outing every year. AllAlloy pledges a donation of S$50 to selected charities for every invited guest who attends the event. In doing so, we aim to engage customers and partners to give back to society in a more meaningful way.

Since 2013, AllAlloy has also extended invitations to social workers and volunteers from supported charities to honour their contributions to society. An annual charity drive was also started in the same year to rally other companies to contribute to charitable causes.

Company Culture

AllAlloy sees itself as a people's company, where success is a collective effort.

This people-centric approach has been pivotal in this young company's achievements. It has also shown that with strong teamwork and continuous innovation, a budding company is still capable of being competitive even amidst strong industry competition.

An Idiom to Describe Your Business

Time and tide wait for no man.

Asia Polyurethane
Mfg Pte Ltd

CEO: Erman TAN

"A lifelong learning culture
must be cultivated
within the organization."

Company Profile

Asia Polyurethane Mfg Pte Ltd (APU), established in 1985, is the first fully-equipped systems house based in the ASEAN region to tailor polyurethane systems to the needs of customers. The Company has grown over the years, guided by the philosophy of providing excellent service and fair and competitive pricing. APU has its headquarters in Singapore, with more than 98% of its sales coming from exporting to more than 42 countries all over the world.

APU's mission is to provide cost-effective, innovative and customised polyurethane solutions by focusing on quality, prompt delivery and technical service and support to enhance productivity and performance.

Significant Milestones

In the last 15 years, APU has managed to establish strong business relations internationally with its footprint found in 42 countries.

Another major milestone was embarking on a research-oriented collaboration with SPRING Singapore, a statutory board under the Ministry of Trade and Industry.

Achieving the Singapore Quality Class, Singapore Innovation Class, Singapore Service Class and People Developer certifications, as well as the subsequent "re-certifications", serves as a testimony to continuous product innovation and quality, diversified service offerings and exemplary people development.

Setbacks

In such a highly competitive market, it is paramount to look into the expansion of the business when the opportunity strikes, says Mr Tan. Unfortunately, due to the lack of talent within the organisation, APU has missed out on some opportunities to venture into new business sectors which would have, otherwise, taken the business to a greater height.

This further reinforces the importance of investing in human capital to ensure that the company remains flexible and ready for future developments. As they reflect on past setbacks, they have also learnt to be more cautious and prudent in the deployment of resources and capital, especially in overseas setups, since operating under different business environments subjects them to different governments and policies.

The setbacks have not set them back, but rather made them stronger and more vigilant.

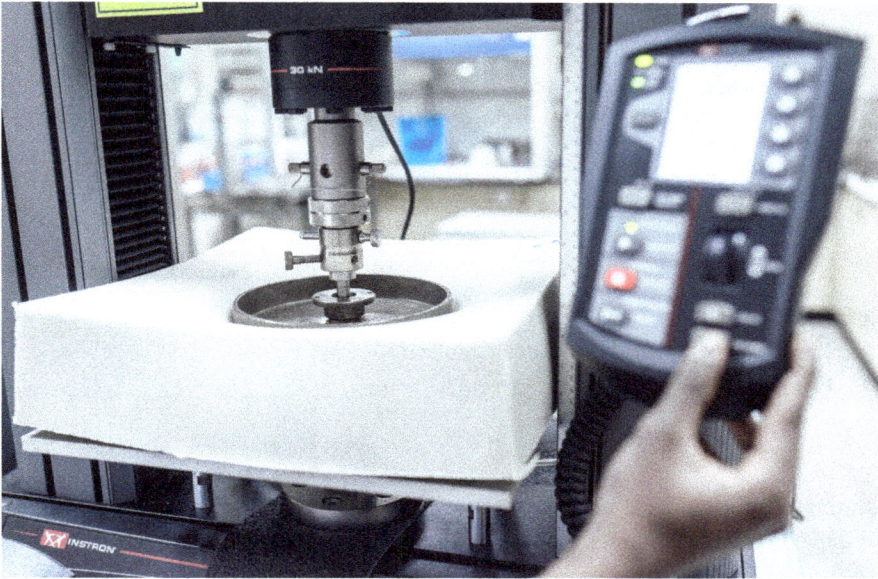

Turning Point

Diversification is key for APU — from both the product and people perspectives.

Diversity at the workplace is essential because, for example, employing people based on merit rather than age, race or ethnicity, has allowed APU to gain more ideas and expertise. A mature team is always able to leverage its experience and knowledge to provide the necessary solutions and avert unnecessary pitfalls, says Mr Tan. This readies the business for rapid expansion. On the other hand, a younger team will be able to offer creative ideas which may allow things to be done differently, and this will aid in the innovation that is very much required in today's competitive world.

"Time and tide wait for no man. We need to be on our toes and quicker than our competitors." Taking his cue from this quote, Mr Tan says the ability to identify new markets and quickly penetrate them (including the Indian sub-continent, the Middle East and Africa) as well as the ability to create new products (in the automotive and oil and gas industries) has fuelled further growth for APU and proven to be significant turning points.

Advice to Budding Entrepreneurs

A lifelong learning culture must be cultivated within the organisation. Whether it is the management or the employees, they need to be imbued with the "Huo dao lao, xue dao lao" spirit. The management must walk the talk by showing their passion, perseverance and attitude towards learning. It is also essential to put knowledge to good use so that new ideas can be generated. Of course, establishing good relationships with other entrepreneurs and networking opportunities which allow for the sharing of best practices will always be vital to both entrepreneurs and their businesses.

Must-have Qualities of Successful Entrepreneurs

- Resilience with a "never say die" attitude
- Receptivity and the "dare to try" mindset
- Be an opportunist with the "just do it" spirit

The Next 50 Years

In the near future, APU needs to establish a wider network in the Middle East as it is a region rich in resources like oil and energy minerals. Having a stronger foothold in the region will enable APU to reduce raw material production costs in the long run. APU needs to tap into these advantages through joint collaborations or acquisitions. The long term aim is to have an edge in competing for quality chemical performance, cost-effectiveness, efficiency and excellence in support and services.

Ultimately "APU" wants to become the Singapore brand name for the chemical industries.

Industry Trends in the Next 50 Years

Due to the increased prices of raw materials, polyurethane (PU) will experience a cost-driven price rise. With the rapid growth in downstream demand, the PU industrial chain will play a role in transferring the cost pressure from rising prices in crude oil. In the PU industrial chain, most products have distinct features, so the output is relatively small and the supply is not quite adequate for the demand. There is great demand and growth potential for serving consumption industries.

The cycled drive of downstream automobile and home appliance industries, as well as the upward trend of PU industrial chains will remain unchanged.

The increased awareness in environmental protection has encouraged many companies to start looking at being more environmentally-friendly and moving towards adopting more energy-saving measures. For example, foam plastics with good fire retardancy will extinguish themselves when there is a small fire. This can reduce the danger of fire spreading and giving out stimulative, toxic smoke. The future PU industry must include the awareness of environmental requirements, such as low levels of smoke, and adopt effective, low-halogen or halogen-free retardants.

Since people are attaching more and more importance on environmental protection, the elimination of pollution and rational exploitation of resources is also regarded as an important problem that needs solutions. As an important high polymer, rational recycling and reusing of PU materials will bring great social and economic benefits.

Major Contributions to the Economy

- APU has innovative and high-value knowledge in the polyurethane industry. This can help enhance the quality and productivity of our economy.
- APU has expanded worldwide and attracted many talents from other regions; this enhances their position as a regional human capital hub.
- APU is able to connect and integrate with different industries internationally and this fosters global integration and development of efficiency and creativity.

Representing Singapore Internationally

- Quality and reliable products and services
- Innovation and creativity
- Customised products and services to meet each customer's needs
- Speedy response to the needs of customers

Major Influence and Inspiration

The fighting spirit and dedication shown in serving their respective countries of both India's independent leader, Mahatma Gandhi, and Singapore's founding father, Mr Lee Kuan Yew, are inspirations to Mr Tan. It is amazing to learn of the less travelled roads they took in overcoming challenges to finally achieve their aims.

As a business owner with accountability to his employees, it is important to stay focused and resilient in the face of any adversity, he added.

Name a Local Dish that Best Represents You or Your Business

Multi-coloured Kueh Lapis — Mr Tan would like to see the different "layers" in Kueh as an embodiment of the values of both APU and himself.

Like Kueh, which requires steaming to be done layer by layer before we can get the final product, we need to have passion and patience in nurturing employees, cultivating good relationships with customers and partners, and growing the business. The different colours add to the attractiveness of the Kueh and also represent the vibrancy and positivity seen in the environment.

Giving Back

As a company, APU believes wholeheartedly in giving back to the community and has incorporated this into the company ethos under the phrase "Work Value".

APU has humble beginnings. Mr Tan says they are thankful to the community and people who have helped and inspired them in one way or another as they built their business. He wants the staff to realise that they should not just have business ethics and commercial objectives, but should also appreciate others and reciprocate their kindness, much like the how the Chinese idiom "Yin shui si yuan" goes.

By promoting the importance of giving back, APU hopes to have employees who are not merely efficient and capable, but who also hold strong values in life. They believe that this will make APU more successful and sustainable in the next 50 years.

Company Culture

APU has a lifelong learning mindset and adopts an open door culture. They believe in empowerment, in being receptive and in hearing feedback from all levels.

An Idiom to Describe Your Business

With insufficient local talent, APU has had to grow the business with greater input from within. Teamwork is crucial. In APU, every employee is valuable. Everybody's contribution is important to the growth of the company. All resources, knowledge and information need to be shared in order to secure the best possible outcomes. Like the growth of a child — the business is a result of every member's contribution. APU lives by the ethos that "it takes a village to raise a child."

"Employees sacrificed by taking a minimum salary of S$400 per month and suppliers were willing to accept longer credit terms."

Company Profile

With the belief that they are no less capable than the big European crane manufacturers, BD Cranetech started business with a mere S$100,000 in paid up capital and five staff on 26 January 1991 as specialists in electric hoist and cranes. Having built their empire over the past 24 years, turnover has multiplied to more than S$25,000,000 and the company has more than 150 employees today.

Over the last 24 years, they have successfully designed and erected standard and special cranes ranging from a capacity of 0.5 tonnes to 1760 tonnes. Additional special cranes include two 600 tonne/hour Shipunloaders for Jurong Port Pte Ltd, a 250 tonne by 85 m span Double Girder Gantry Crane for Keppel Singmarine, a 20 tonne by 96 m span Single Girder Gantry Crane for the erection of a six storey building for Manufacture Element Prefabricate Pte Ltd and a 1760 tonne Gantry hoisting platform for Penta-Ocean to carry out Geo-tube Reclamation in PSA Pasir Pajang.

Significant Milestones

- Securing the first order from an MNC company two months after starting business.
- Surviving the cashflow crisis and making a return to re-organise/structure with new business strategies.
- Being an Enterprise 50 winner — confirmation and endorsement of their business success.

Memorable Setbacks

The burgeoning company ran into a cashflow situation from 2001 to 2003. They were awarded a project to supply two Shipunloaders to Jurong Port. When the payment did not follow in accordance with the projected timeline, they ran into a cashflow situation. BD Cranetech only managed to pull through with the support of the employees and suppliers. Employees sacrificed by taking a minimum salary of S$400 per month and suppliers were willing to grant much longer credit terms to repay the amount owed to them.

The lesson BD Cranetech learnt was that cashflow planning is very critical for any business to survive.

Turning Point

The huge turning point for the business came when they became business partners with ASL Marine and Keppel Singmarine. BD Cranetech's experience and exposure

in various businesses gave them the platform to prove their worth to their partners in their yard planning and development projects. This included the work flow, factory layout, type of cranes to use and other facilities. With the success of this strategy, many clients have subsequently approached the company for similar setup models.

Advice to Budding Entrepreneurs

Think of how you can value add to your client. Be wise in cash flow planning and have enough perseverance to overcome all difficulties.

Must-have Qualities of a Successful Entrepreneur

- Be an expert in the field of business
- Be innovative in creating value for your clients
- Always strive to excel

The Next 50 Years

BD Cranetech expects to be further established as a well-known and reputable Singapore brand globally. The type of cranes designed and produced will not be limited to just Electric Overhead Cranes and Gantry Cranes but also Cranes for the Oil and Gas Industries, Marine Cranes, Automated Port Handling Cranes and other special cranes to meet customers' needs.

There will also be research done on designing cranes whereby the end user can assemble them much like fixing lego pieces together.

Industry-specific — In the future, crane requirements will be for higher capacity, longer span and higher lifting height. The cranes will be designed based on new materials and technology such that the structural weight will be lighter and assembly will be easier. New intelligent control systems will allow the operator to operate the crane more easily, hence increasing productivity. The price of cranes will also be cheaper because of improved technology.

Major Contributions to the Economy

- Transforming from a conventional to a modern and innovative manufacturing provider in a heavy industry.
- With the transformation, customers are able to benefit from increased productivity and efficiency and hence increase their business by more than two times. In return, it increased the number of orders in BD Cranetech's order book.
- A new supply chain surrounding the business has been formed.

Representing Singapore Internationally

Being the only original equipment manufacturer in Singapore and Southeast Asia that has the ability to design and manufacture cranes of up to 1760 tonne capacities, BD Cranetech products are comparable to European and American products in terms of quality, yet competitive with Chinese players in terms of pricing. This is proven by the cranes they have sold to countries in the Middle East, Brazil, the USA, Vietnam and China.

Major Influence and Inspiration

Mr Lim cites Mr Lee Kuan Yew and his bravery and determination in making the impossible, possible for Singapore. This was done by gaining the trust of his cabinet to strive, commit and forge ahead.

Name a Local Dish that Best Represents You and Your Business

Tze char — The wide variety of dishes cater to customers' choices and require fresh ingredients and a good chef to serve up inexpensive, quality and delectable dishes. BD Cranetech needs to be flexible and creative to meet customers' requests for special dishes, like Hor Fun with fresh oysters, that are not on the menu and also deliver them at reasonable prices. It is also important to constantly improve old dishes and introduce new ones in order to both maintain old customers and attract new ones.

Company Culture

With a mission to demonstrate sincerity and genuine interest in everything they do, BD Cranetech are constantly looking for ways to exceed client expectations and to help clients succeed by offering them solutions that are of tremendous value.

An Idiom to Describe Your Business

忍辱负重，严己宽人! Swallow humiliation and bear a heavy load; bear disgrace and a heavy burden; bear responsibility and blame; discharge one's duties conscientiously in spite of slanders; endure humiliation in order to carry out an important mission; grin and bear it.

"Hold yourself responsible to a higher standard than anybody else expects of you. Never excuse yourself. Never pity yourself. Be a hard master to yourself — and be lenient to everybody else."

Henry Ward Beecher

Company Profile

Bengawan Solo was founded in 1979 by Tjendri Anastasia, who is originally from Indonesia. Anastasia came to Singapore where she met her husband, Johnson Liew. After getting married, her interest in Indonesian delicacies, honed during her growing up years, continued in the little home kitchen of her HDB flat. Gradually, word of the existence of her tasty goodies got around, and before she knew it, orders for her cakes and kueh came rolling in. Her home-made specialties even made it onto the shelves of some supermarkets and emporiums, albeit produced without a food manufacturing licence.

Significant Milestones

From the start up, Bengawan Solo's early growth period between 1979 and 1990 was rapid. By this time, the firm had 12 outlets, 100 employees and three key staff who helped Mrs Liew, the owner-entrepreneur. This entrepreneurial style which built up a strong foundation for Bengawan Solo, is characterised by factors such as creativity, innovation (e.g. constantly introducing new recipes and improving existing ones), and risk-taking.

However this period also witnessed the owner assuming responsibility for all phases of the firm's operations. Mrs Liew took charge of production, sales, personnel, accounting, finance, product design and development, advertising, purchasing and all other aspects of day-to-day business.

Setbacks

When officials from the Ministry of Environment finally caught up with her and her unlicensed food production, she was warned and instructed to stop her home baking business. The incident turned out to be a blessing in disguise as it led to Mrs Liew's decision to set up the very first Bengawan Solo Cake Shop in Marine Terrace.

Qualities of a Successful Entrepreneur

The basics of Mrs Liew's business is that "she had a recipe" coupled with good business acumen, sheer hard work and perseverance, especially during the initial years when she had to handle everything. She has also always loved challenges. In particular, she is armed with specialised culinary skills in making traditional Indonesian and local kueh and cakes.

As an entrepreneur, she maintains high standards for her products to maintain goodwill. Even at later stages when products were produced in a centralised kitchen, she continued her traditional methods of production, used the finest ingredients and prepared her deliveries without preservatives. She is always firm in her principles, and has never and will never cut corners or sell products that are not fresh. A perfectionist, Mrs Liew's business philosophy is that every task, whether in retail outlets or the centralised kitchen, must be performed perfectly, or nearest perfection. Likewise, for every item of Indonesian and local kueh or cake, she insists on making it better than others.

The Future

Bengawan Solo Cake Shop started from nothing when Mrs Liew opened her first outlet in 1979. Like all other cake shops in Singapore at that time, production was carried out in the kitchen at the back of a small shop-house of a block of HDB flats. Eight years later with five outlets in operation, the little shop-house space was bursting at the seams, which then prompted her to build her first central kitchen on a 9500 square foot piece of private property at Harvey Road in the MacPherson area. Her centralised factory production was featured several times in the local papers as it was the first of its kind in the confectionery industry and was later emulated by others in the business.

In November 1997, with 25 outlets, the company shifted its central kitchen to a 25,000 square foot factory in Woodlands. The investment was then about six million dollars and this present factory is expected to meet the expansionary needs of the company for the next few years. To date, Bengawan Solo has a total of 38 retail outlets and more than 409 employees.

Borden Company Pte Ltd

MD: Christopher YEO

"Different industries offer different sets of challenges and so entrepreneurs must have a vision and mission for their business."

Company Profile

Borden Company (Pte) Ltd is a Singaporean pharmaceutical manufacturing company which has been around since 1960. It produces the well-known Eagle Brand Medicated Oil, which has become synonymously known as the "Green Oil" and renowned for its fragrance, healing and soothing properties.

Eagle Brand medicated oil was formulated in 1935 by a German chemist for J Lea & Co, a trading house owned by the late Mr Tan Jim Lay, a direct descendant of the patriarch Mr Tan Quee Lan. He was a well-known Chinese merchant and philanthropist in Singapore during the early 1900's. The Eagle Brand medicated oil under J Lea & Co flourished and grew significantly and dominated the local market for medicated oil in the post-war period.

In 1960, the late Mr Tan Jim Lay got together a few of his business associates to join his company as shareholders in order to strengthen the capital base and fortify the management of the business. Borden Co. Pte Ltd was officially incorporated on the 26th of March 1960 to take over the business of J Lea & Co, including the Eagle Brand trade mark and the proprietary rights acquired from Wilhelm Hauffmann & Company. In 1963, Borden Co. Pte Ltd formally registered Wilhelm Hauffmann & Company as a business name under its sole ownership.

Although the medicated oil remains the flagship product, a quest to be resilient as well as to capitalise on brand equity and research and development has led to the creation of an extended range of pharmaceutical products, such as medicated balms, eucalyptus oils, muscle rubs, plasters, and disinfectant sprays and swipes, in order to better cater to the changing needs and expectations of consumers.

Setbacks

One of the biggest challenges for the business is overcoming counterfeits in overseas markets due to the overwhelming popularity of the products. This is especially so in third world countries where the trademark laws are more lax. In an effort to curb the counterfeits, Borden took the bold step of changing their packaging adopted for the last 50 years, and made improvements to them by incorporating 3-D holograms with security features so that it is harder for unscrupulous businessmen to imitate. A second approach is to work with the local authorities in consistently conducting raids based on ground information that are obtained via distributors or private investigators.

Although there has been a decline in the counterfeit products in the market after these measures were implemented, it is an on-going battle to weed out this problem.

Advice to Budding Entrepreneurs

Different industries offer different sets of challenges and as a start for entrepreneurs, one must have a vision and mission for your business. At the same time, be positive and set realistic goals to be achieved within a stipulated time frame and review them occasionally. Be focused and never lose sight of the objectives that you have set out to achieve at different stages of your business. Do not be discouraged even when things do not turn out the way that you may have planned it to be. Instead, be prepared to persevere and re-evaluate the situation before planning the next move. Do not get too complacent even if you attain some form of success in the first attempt. Instead, continue to build on the momentum to scale greater heights to achieve more. Lastly, always be humble and be mindful of the people around you who may have in one way or another helped you in your quest to be an entrepreneur.

Must-have Qualities of Successful Entrepreneurs

- Passion: One must be passionate about the business or goals that they are pursuing and at the same time enjoy the learning process that comes with growing the business.
- Tenacity: One must also be committed to put in 200% of their effort and be "hungry" for success. It is only with sheer tenacity that one will be motivated to succeed.
- Perseverance: To always maintain a positive mindset and "can do" attitude in overcoming challenges and obstacles along the way that are at times beyond one's control. Even if one fails on their first attempt, one should never be discouraged but should instead continue to try again.

Turning Point

It would have to be the founders' vision and ambition to look beyond our shores after having established a foothold in the local market of the medicated oil industry in the 1960s. Their foresight of venturing overseas subsequently led to establishing market presence in more than 20 countries globally as well as brand loyalty amongst consumers in many countries. However, the success of the company is also credited to the unrelenting commitment of the current generation of top management to capitalise on its branding and innovate, thus developing a whole range of products to cater to the changing needs and demands of consumers today. Their adherance to the business virtues of hard work and sincerity, along with contributions and dedication of every member of the company and the commitment

and strong close ties with valued partners and distributors, as well as loyal consumers' unwavering trust and confidence in the brand and products, is significant in the company's continued success.

Significant Milestones

In 2006, Eagle Brand was accorded the SPBA Heritage Brand Award by the Association of Small Medium Enterprise (ASME). The award is given to brands that have been established for more than 25 years in Singapore as well as having evidence that the branding has significantly contributed to the growth and the development of the brand.

In 2006, the single-storey detached factory was redeveloped into a 50,000 square feet purpose-built new seven-storey light industrial building conforming with cGMP specification equipped with the latest pharmaceutical manufacturing and testing machineries, as well as with a showroom-cum-office and warehouse under one roof. With the new manufacturing facility, the factory was able to increase its production by up to three-fold and also now has the capacity to accommodate another 100% increase.

In 2014, Borden Company was accorded the Top Honours of the Enterprise 50 Awards by *The Business Times* and KPMG. The Enterprise 50 Awards recognises contributions that local, privately-held companies have made to economic

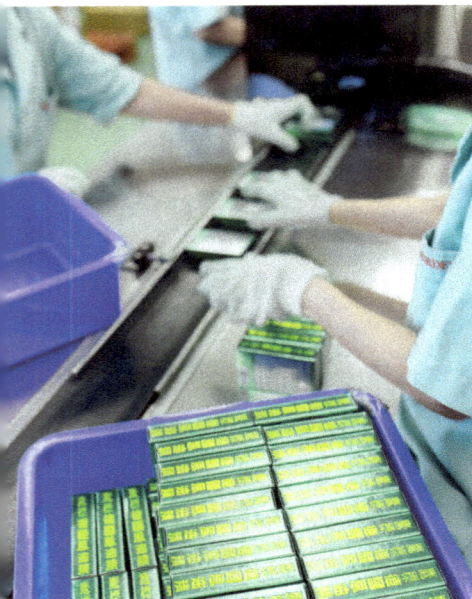

development in Singapore and abroad. It also embodies the finest in Singapore entrepreneurship and exemplifies the spirit of innovation, entrepreneurship and the true strength of enterprise. As such, to be accorded an Enterprise 50 award, is a testament to the accomplishments of an SME in Singapore and serves as a launching platform in raising the company's profile in their effort to expand into new markets.

The Next 50 Years

Many people believe that this is a sunset industry but Borden begs to differ. Self-medication through external analgesics is still widely sought after amongst people living in third world countries as well as in developed countries, be it via oils, creams, rubs or patches. As a matter of fact, the business has been growing steadily over the last 55 years and the company aspires to continue soaring to greater heights for many years to come.

Being a pioneer in the manufacturing of external analgesics, through R & D, they are able to efficiently innovate and develop new products that cater to the changing consumers' needs and high expectations, capitalising on the heritage brand that they have built over the years.

Although the medicated oil remains their core product and accounts for about 85% of the revenue for the company, dedicated research and development has created an extended range of pharmaceutical products, such as medicated balms, eucalyptus oils, muscle rubs, plasters, and disinfectant sprays and swipes, amongst others.

Armed with a whole range of external analgesics that cater to consumers of all ages, the growth opportunities for the company looks promising as this industry is believed to be recession-proof. In order to grow, Borden has to remain focused and nurture the markets where they have garnered a strong presence. Markets where they may not be strong or are a new entrant in, offer even greater growth opportunities to grow the consumer base and position themselves to take some market share away from competitors through aggressive marketing and branding campaigns.

They also remain committed to innovating new quality products every two years in a bid to remain resilient and competitive.

Industry Trends in the Next 50 Years

Over the years, Borden has noticed that people, both young and old, are more conscious about their diets and also have a desire to lead a healthier lifestyle. More people are taking up healthy lifestyles by engaging in some form of physical activities such as running, swimming, cycling or even playing a sport competitively. In the course of engaging in such activities, one may be plagued with superficial aches and pains that do not require medical attention but nonetheless, could seek some form of pain relief through external analgesics.

Borden believes that the demand for such analgesics will continue to grow in the years to come as more young people resort to healthy living by exercising regularly in their quest to stay fit and live longer.

As manufacturers of external analgesics, they remain committed to innovating new high quality pain relief remedies to keep up with the demand and expectations of younger groups of consumers.

Major Contributions to the Economy

For manufacturers of any industry, it is always a challenge for companies to keep operating costs down in order to improve the bottom line. As such, many would take the initiative to relocate their manufacturing facilities to countries where they are able to get cheap labour and rental in order to keep costs down.

Borden prides themselves as a home-grown pharmaceutical manufacturer, having the products manufactured out of their facility here and remain committed to doing so for generations to come. With about 90% of business exported globally, they remain a key exporter of a "Made in Singapore" pharmaceutical brand for external analgesics.

Over the years, in an effort to improve productivity, they have embarked on the implementation of automated machineries so as to be less reliant on manpower. However, they continue to retain their workforce, mostly locals and retirees, for less laborious work required in the manufacturing process so as to create jobs for the industry.

Representing Singapore Internationally

Having achieved a foothold in the local market, the founders then had a vision and ambition to venture overseas. The product was first introduced in Vietnam in the 1960s, and has since gained overwhelming popularity and acceptance amongst the Vietnamese. In the local Vietnamese household, the "Green Oil" is widely accepted as a common cure-all household remedy and a "must have" item. Further in

Vietnam, the "Green Oil" has attained a status whereby it is widely given and sought as a premium gift item during festive and joyous occasions due to its unique fragrance and cure-all remediable use.

Earlier investment plans to start a manufacturing facility to produce the "Green Oil" in Vietnam in the 1970's was aborted due to the outbreak of the Vietnam War in 1975. However, as a result of the war, the newly established Vietnamese enclaves in North America, Continental Europe and Australasia created new demand and markets in these new locations for Eagle Brand Medicated Oil.

Throughout the years, Eagle Brand Medicated Oil has established its presence and availability in many countries. The impetus was the migration of the Vietnamese people that brought the oil to other shores. Sales then grew steadily in the countries with strong Vietnamese communities. With such strong demand, Eagle Brand Medicated Oil then started to strengthen further.

Today, Eagle Brand Medicated Oil is sold in more than 20 countries globally and is a drug listed for sale by notable governing health authorities such as the US Food and Drug Administration (FDA) and Australia Therapeutic Goods Administration (TGA).

Positioned as a premium-grade medicated oil, Eagle Brand Medicated Oil has successfully built upon its branding and achieved consumer brand loyalty in countries around the world, thus enjoying market leader status in many countries.

Major Influence and Inspiration

CEO Mr Yeo is constantly inspired by the many success stories of people from all walks of life. Some of their achievements are immeasurable in terms of monetary value, but behind each success is a lesson that one can learn from or be influenced by.

Name a Local Dish that Best Represents You or Your Business

To Mr Yeo, Teochew porridge best represents the business as it is a simple dish that's been served for generations and remains a favourite amongst many today. Similarly, Borden and their products have been resilient and trusted for generations due to their premium quality and efficacy.

Giving Back

In Mr Yeo's opinion, all companies should try to inculcate the spirit of giving back to the community within its own capacity by making contributions to charitable organisations that take care of the less privileged and the needy. Any form of support will never be deemed too small as long as we are prepared to share our blessings with the less fortunate.

As part of Borden's contribution to the community, Borden has also adopted a 12 feet high Eagle statue and an American Bald Eagle at the Jurong Bird Park since 2006 in support of the preservation of bird life. Over the years, they have also been approached by various organisations for donations and have made numerous contributions-in-kind with products as well as cash donations to the less privileged. In conjunction with Eagle Brand's 80th anniversary this year, donations were also made to SINDA, the AMP – Ready for School Fund and Singhealth Foundation

Company Culture

The company's current setup consists of beneficiaries of the second & third generations of the original founding families and operates like a big family business. As in many family-run businesses, the success lies in the cohesiveness and mutual respect amongst the team members within the organisation.

Many loyal staff have also been with the company for many years, ranging from ten years to the longest serving of 47 years! The main reason why they continue working with the company is because they believe in the integrity and fair practices of the company. In addition, it has been the company's philosophy to share the fruits of its labour with every member of the establishment.

And in celebration of Borden Company's 50th Anniversary in 2010, the company rewarded staff with a six-day "World Expo Tour 2010" to China as a token of appreciation for their contribution and dedication.

In March 2013, the company also incentivised staff with a six-day Tour of Taiwan for achieving another great year of success in 2012.

An Idiom to Describe Your Business

Unity is Strength!

"The silver lining was that we were not too bogged down by how other people were doing business."

Company Profile

Capita is a recruitment and talent management company providing staffing and search services. The company's six divisions cover various industry functions and specialisations — Capita Business Support places professionals in corporate support positions such as human resources & administration, accounting & finance, sales & marketing and logistics & supply chain. Capita Technology covers the IT & telco industry and also has divisions catering to placements for Banking, Engineering and Healthcare roles, as well as an Outsourcing division that does temporary and contract staffing.

Challenges

The early days were a challenge as CEO Mr Koh came into the business with little or no knowledge – akin to a blank piece of paper, as he puts it. He had highly underestimated what was required to build up the business. "We basically plunged into the business so we did not come in with fixed processes, systems nor a wealth of experience on how this business had to be done," says Mr Koh. This was quite challenging in the sense that, throughout the initial years, they had to develop their own systems and processes from scratch. The silver lining was that they were not too bogged down by how other people were doing business. They created their own processes based on the values that they believed in and carved out their own niche – the Capita Way of doing things.

Staff retention was another major challenge. Capita had to be very deliberate in their actions and manage people at the same time. "I treat people as my most valuable assets so my every action and how I relate to them is very important. They are not just my employees; they are my partners. Just like how our principles define how we treat our employees — it is about mutual respect, responsibility and partnership. I am fortunate to have most of my pioneer team members with us today," said Mr Koh.

Advice to Budding Entrepreneurss

First, decide whether you want to be in it or not. Decide whether you really want to be an entrepreneur. If you decide to have a business, have a very clear dream or goal and believe in it.

Then, take very practical actions to make things happen and make sure you achieve it. Big plans mean nothing without execution. One of the most important things is to take practical actions that support your growth and positively impact your business/bottom line. Do not just do the things that others seem to be doing.

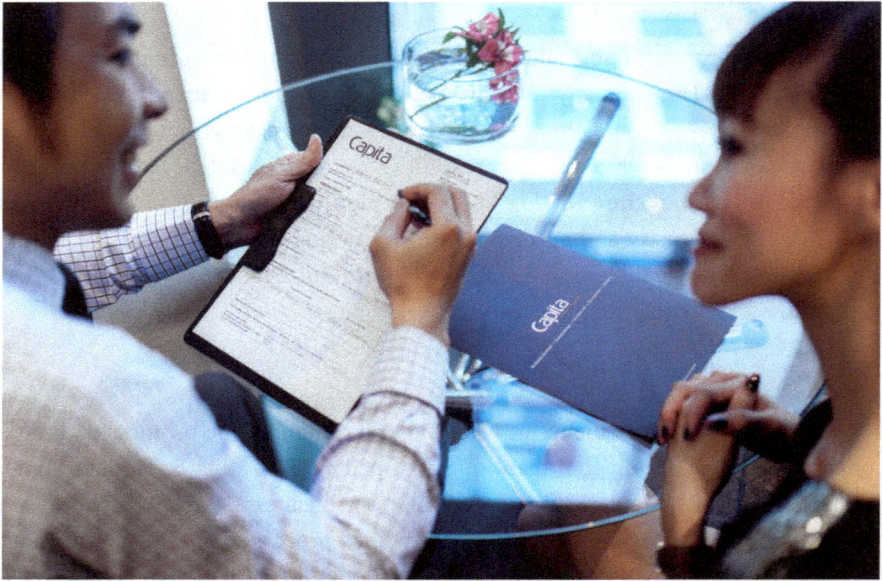

You need to really persevere and focus to ensure that you see the end result. A lot of people give up midway, just before they get the results. Tenacity and perseverance are the keys to success.

Must-have Qualities of Successful Entrepreneurs

The will to make things happen is important. The will and desire to succeed, the mindset, the desire to make things happen. When you have the will and the tenacity to do something or succeed, you will eventually find your way.

Adaptability and flexibility. Many times, things do not go according to plan. You need to be constantly flexible and adaptable, be on the go and readjust, refocus each and every day. While you should be steadfast in pursuing your dreams and goals, you should also be flexible in your execution.

Be humble. This is the most important trait. Only by being humble yet confident, can you then learn from your surroundings, mentors, people who work with you and your colleagues.

Turning Point

In 2008, when the financial crisis hit, it proved to be one of the company's biggest challenges. That was when the reality of running a business with a responsibility to his people really hit home, says Mr Koh. "I really had to drill down and understand the business seriously — what works and what does not work, what steps to take every day, how to manage cash flow and how to turn things around faster. I did not only have to fight for survival, we also had to plan and take some calculated risks to grow our company during that time," he says. The lessons learnt then and the culture built since has allowed them to scale the company to what it is today.

Significant Milestones

Mr Koh thinks his greatest achievement is his people. At least 80% of his initial pioneer team is still with him today and some have also been around for more than five or six years, despite the company only being eight years in the business.

Secondly, their brand is recognised in the industry with the ASME-Rotary Entrepreneur of the Year Award (2012), the Enterprise 50 Award (2012) as well as the Spirit of Enterprise Award (2013), amongst other industry accolades. These awards have given confidence despite Capita being a young company and they have provided a local born-and-bred SME like Capita, some credibility in the market to compete with the MNCs.

The third important milestone was when Capita took the step to venture out of Singapore in 2012 into Malaysia. This marked the first overseas testbed for the systems they had developed out of Singapore, and it has done well so far.

The Next 50 Years

In the next 50 years, Singapore and Asia will be a very important hub for services and also talent management and development. Mr Koh hopes to see Capita take advantage of the growth of these industries in Asia and develop into a strong regional player in the recruitment and HR services industry. He thinks there should be a global recruitment MNC developed out of Asia and probably Singapore where local players like Capita have already started to mature in their operations and brand.

In the next 50 years, talent management will be constantly evolving. There will be a greater trend of outsourcing of non-core functions, talent will be more mobile and may not belong to just a single company. Recent changes in the talent industry have seen some companies in the forefront adopting "holacracy" – where people in the company are self-managed instead of reporting to managers in a hierarchy. Mr Koh thinks the next 50 years will see an interesting shift in the development of new HR practices. "I strongly believe that HR services companies like ours will evolve to provide newer and better talent management services."

Representing Singapore Internationally

Capita wants to be able to partner the country in its regional growth. With many more local MNCs and similar small and medium sized enterprises venturing into popular regional zones in Southeast Asia, Capita has expanded its footprint into Asia, starting with Kuala Lumpur, one of the most vibrant cities in the world.

The company is currently in the midst of conducting market research for its foray into other regions and hopes to open more offices in two other Asian countries such as Taiwan, China and Japan in the next two years.

With Asia being one of the most important economies in the world, there will be a great demand for talent in this part of the world. Capita envisions itself taking advantage of the growth of the region's talent industry to become a truly regional/global company that can compete with MNCs in the region and internationally in the future.

Major Influences and Inspirations

Mr Koh's early influence and inspiration are his parents. They run businesses and have inspired him to want to do something on his own. His father showed him that relentlessness, perseverance and hard work are the keys to success.

Currently, he does not have a single major influence or inspiration but he enjoys reading biographies on how leaders and successful people work and adapts these different inspirations and perspectives into something that could be relevant in his life.

Name a Local Dish that Best Represents You or Your Business

Spring roll. Simple, humble and a dish that is enjoyed by people all over the world. Mr Koh believes this represents his vision of being humble and staying true to his roots, yet with the ability and mission to be truly international and relevant to people regardless of nationality.

Giving Back

Capita is in the human capital industry and believes strongly in the nurturing of talents, starting with the youth. They believe that children are the pillars of the future and Capita have thus embarked on corporate social responsibility efforts towards children's causes.

For example, the company has participated actively in the 1000 Enterprises for Children-in-Need project, committing as the lead sponsor in the project for a period of three years.

They intend to expand their corporate social responsibility efforts in other projects, including giving career talks in schools and providing students with free career guidance.

Company Culture

Capita describes their company culture as closely knit. This is based predominantly on the three principles that they want employees to adopt — mutual respect, responsibility and partnership. "I believe that successful team work, collaboration and communication will allow the company to go far, as these are the values that bring people to work together to move to the next level in both personal and business development," says Mr Koh.

An Idiom to Describe Your Business

Mr Koh loves this quote which he believes captures the essence of the culture in the company. People are the only asset in the business after all.

> *"Regard your soldiers as your children, and they will follow you into the deepest valleys. Look on them as your own beloved sons, and they will stand by you even unto death!"*

Sun Tzu, quote from the Art of War

CarTimes Automobile Pte Ltd

CEO Eddie LOO

"A positive mindset and maintaining a clear vision for the future go a long way in getting through turbulent times."

The Business

Incorporated in 2001, CarTimes Automobile is Singapore's leading company for brand new and pre-owned cars. In 2005, just four years after the company started operations, CarTimes became the first automotive company to be accorded the highly-prestigious Enterprise 50 Award. In 2006, the company also won the Singapore Promising Brand Award and achieved the Singapore 1000 Highest Sales Turnover Award in retail.

The company's core business is in the following areas: Pre-Owned Cars (Japanese and Continental), New Cars (parallel import), Car Grooming, Car Financing and Car Insurance. From 2012 onwards, the company is embarking on an aggressive regional expansion plan that will take it beyond the shores of Singapore in search of sustainable growth.

Setbacks

A tipping point for the company happened in its first two years of business. A perfect storm of several major events came together — COE prices dropping to as low as S$101, September 11 (9/11) and the outbreak of SARS. The car industry was severely hit.

To make things worse, a year after establishment, one of the founding partners had a change of heart and withdrew from the business, taking with him a crucial source of capital already in the business. Concurrently, the company found its left hand chopped off when a quarter of CarTimes' staff were headhunted by their competitors.

The odds were stacked against CarTimes and founder, Mr Eddie Loo. Times like these taught them strong lessons on the need for perseverance, not to be too complacent and the importance of recognising that good times don't last forever. Most importantly, Mr Loo learnt the importance of treasuring the staff who stood by the company through tough times.

Advice to Budding Entrepreneurs

Mr Loo feels strongly about believing in yourself, cultivating a fearless spirit and a never-say-die attitude. Having a positive mindset and maintaining a clear vision for the future also go a long way in getting through turbulent periods.

Major Turning Point

In 2003, the car industry started to improve and along with it the fortunes of CarTimes. In just two years, in 2005, Mr Loo, its managing director, became the

first person in the industry to be awarded the coveted 'Entrepreneur of the Year Award', a national award for local entrepreneurs who have demonstrated excellence in their field and who have significantly contributed to Singapore's economy and society. In addition, CarTimes also became the first automotive company to be listed in the Enterprise 50, as one of the fastest growing companies in Singapore.

The Future

CarTimes aims to be a listed company on the SGX, branching out into the Asia Pacific, becoming a full-fledged automobile business, which includes: selling-buying of new and pre-owned cars, rental, and workshops.

Greater emphasis will also be given to moving business online, in line with industry trends as consumers become more tech-savvy. Another emphasis will be on customer relationship management services.

In the next 50 years, the industry will also move toward a higher level of transparency, while greater competition will also mean companies have to provide more personalised services as customers' expectations continue to rise. Technological advances mean new features such as those that allow customers to customise their cars online.

Major Contributions to Singapore

- Social responsibility
- Contribution to Gross Domestic Product (GDP)
- Providing jobs

Representing Singapore Internationally

CarTimes seeks to espouse the Singaporean values of trust and integrity, as a homegrown car company.

Major Influence and Inspiration

Mr Lee Kuan Yew. His charismatic leadership, vision and far-sightedness stand as a model of integrity and transformed Singapore from a third world country to a first world nation.

Name a Local Dish that Best Represents You or Your Business

Chicken rice. CarTimes is able to provide a wide range of cars from luxury to mass market, family-oriented ones to suit the needs of a wider range of customers.

The cucumbers, chilli and dark sauce that are added on to the dish represent the breadth of knowledge that a CarTimes salesman possesses, which allows quality services to be delivered with a warm smile.

Giving Back

CarTimes has participated in numerous charities and events.

*Charity event with
Mr Lee Kuan Yew*

*Charity event with
Mr Goh Chok Tong*

*SVTA Bursary Award with
Mr Tharman Shanmugaratnam*

*Annual National Arthritis Foundation
Charity Golf (Hole-In-One sponsor)*

*Annual Kidz Horizon Charity Golf
(Hole-In-One sponsor)*

Company Culture

CarTimes abides by brand values such as integrity, professionalism, teamwork and genuineness.

These values are core factors contributing to the success of CarTimes.

An Idiom to Describe Your Business

Time to Smile.

Cyclect Group

MD: Melvin TAN

"With passion as your primary ingredient, have your checklist of other ingredients for success handy."

Company Profile

Established in 1943, Cyclect is a group of engineering services companies, serving diverse markets and operating in nine countries. They provide Engineering, Procurement, Construction and Maintenance solutions for Offshore, Marine, Infrastructure, Industry, Energy and Building segments. Their core services include mechanical, electrical, controls and instrumentation. A diverse clientele includes the iconic Formula 1 Singapore Grand Prix, Universal Studios, Exxon Mobil, Shell, Energizer, Pfizer, Samsung, Marina Bay Sands and Singapore Sports Hub amongst many others. Cyclect is a recipient of multiple awards including Enterprise 50, PMO Innovator, Singapore Sustainability Awards, Business Superbrands, Singapore Prestige Brand Awards, ASEAN Best Electrical Contractor and ASEAN Business Awards.

Significant Milestones

In 2000, Cyclect established an innovation team. They focused on applications of innovations for the aviation industry, homeland defense against chemical attacks and clean energy. They were recognised for their efforts when they were awarded the Innovator Award under the Prime Minister's Office twice. For their clean energy business, they were recognized as a winner in the Singapore Sustainability Awards 2012 and Asean Business Awards for Innovation 2014 which was presented by the President of Myanmar.

In 2003 during a moment of enormous challenge, they also found opportunity. Opportunity to transform the company, to change established practices and to renew the company. They changed bankers, groomed new leaders and diversified their portfolio.

In 2008, they were honoured with the award of the Singapore GP Formula 1 project to design and build the electrical systems for the inaugural night race. It was an engineering and construction challenge to work on such a mission critical project that the world was watching. It placed them on the map as a credible and reliable partner for engineering services.

Setbacks

For Cyclect, the most turbulent years were from 2003–2006. Cyclect faced a series of unfortunate events caused by the almost perfect storm of SARS, a poor economy and legacy decisions.

- Storm 1: SARS caused the economy on the whole to be severely impacted. Projects were few, and those that were on, had experienced very poor progress, resulting in severe cash flow shortages.

- Storm 2: One of their director's personal business in F&B failed. However, due to contractual complications, it affected Cyclect's primary banker who withdrew its support not only to her personal F&B business, but the whole group. Cash flow was additionally strained.
- Storm 3: To make matters worse, a key member of management was poached by a key client; resulting in a loss of almost 50% of turnover.

It was at this juncture that Mr Tan was promoted from a Business Development Manager role to a General Director, tasked to recover the company from the brink of bankruptcy.

Turning Point

In Mr Tan's family history with the business, they had many turning points. For the founder, it was the Japanese occupation of Singapore. Without that incident, he would have remained an employee. For the second generation, it was when the founder passed away. The current chairman was an unprepared leader and was left with a huge undertaking of running a business.

For Melvin, the crisis of 2003 gave him an opportunity to consolidate the business, build new bonds with the team and to create a new future for the company. They created an innovation team, focused on more profitable but challenging projects and expanded regionally.

Several Lessons Learnt

- The Hedgehog principle: Borrowed from an ancient Greek parable, "The fox knows many things, but the hedgehog knows one big thing." Cyclect had to focus on one thing, engineering service, rather than try to be in a non-related business.
- Determination is a key ingredient to overcome obstacles. There are many ingredients to success in overcoming obstacles; Melvin learnt that determination is one of the primary ingredients.
- Know your banker, let him know you too. Bankers can help, but they can also destroy and mess things up if they fail to know you.
- Have more than one basket for your eggs. Cyclect depended too much on one team, one client, one area of business. When it collapsed, it almost brought the entire building with it. All business should learn to diversify effectively.

Advice to Budding Entrepreneurs

First, you'd definitely need to have passion for the craft or trade. If profit and wealth is your only driver, you'd have to reconsider. With passion as your primary ingredient, have your checklist of other ingredients for success handy. Consider funding, capability, market access amongst the long list of ingredients. You will be blazing a new trail, thus oftentimes you'd have to make tough decisions where you don't have the right resources and information. As Ralph Waldo Emerson said: "Do not go where the path may lead; go instead where there is no path and leave a trail."

Must-have Qualities of Successful Entrepreneurs

- Tenacity and risk tolerance: Moving from having an idea to actually making money takes relentless tenacity. You've got to get up every morning and keep moving the business. The entrepreneur must also be able to accept that they will not have the security of a monthly salary.
- Unwavering passion: You need a deep, irrevocable commitment to your vision and be able to articulate it effectively to gain followers and clients.
- Creativity and intuition: You'd have to trail blaze, making decisions where you don't have all the right information, working with limited resources, thinking of new ideas to solve problems and identifying opportunities.

The Next 50 Years

Mr Tan sees Cyclect as a company that is a force for good. Values of innovation, togetherness, integrity, determination and excellence, will be key drivers. The company believes that profit follows the implementation of their key values.

In the next 50 years, Cyclect aims to continue building on the vision of being a one-stop engineering solutions organisation in ASEAN. However, they plan to develop expertise and apply robotics, big data and analytics and additive manufacturing to the industries they serve.

Industry Trends in the Next 50 Years

Mr Tan believes the world in 50 years will be starkly different from today. Information and electricity will drive the future. It is even possible that demand for marine and air shipping may become non-essential. As robotics, additive manufacturing and high bandwidth data transmission is made available, we can manufacture anything anywhere. Cyclect doesn't have to manufacture in a back room in China and ship it across the world to Australia. The designs are simply sent digitally and printed on a high speed printer and assembled by robots in anyone's backyard, from electronics to clothes.

In the area of energy, he believes it will be primarily from renewable sources where we can harness the sun and store the energy in high density storage systems. This will impact the oil and gas industry which will see further decline in the next decades. In 50 years, it is possible to see the start of the end of fossil fuels.

Major Contributions to the Economy

Cyclect has contributed in a small way to the economy, says Mr Tan.

In the early years, Singapore's main industry was shipping. Cyclect provided ship repairs and supported the economy by ensuring that there is a reliable partner in Singapore to get things done on the vessels. They pride themselves in always getting the job done.

Since 1943, thousands of employees have come through their doors. Cyclect has helped families locally and abroad achieve a better quality of life.

Representing Singapore Internationally

Cyclect is a firm that has represented Singapore since its inception. The earliest customers were multi-national shipping companies from China, Iran, Britain, Japan and the United States. To international clients, Cyclect provides them with a peace of mind, a symbol of a reliable anchor here in the far east.

Today, Cyclect still serves Singapore and international companies regionally. They carry the Singapore flag proudly in nine countries, representing Singapore in various international associations.

They also represent Singapore at international conferences as they present research findings to the international community. Winning the Asean Business Awards for Innovation in 2014 was also a proud achievement.

Major Influence and Inspiration

Mr Lee Kuan Yew. His determination, tenacity, intellect, love and faith for Singapore is inspiring.

Name a Local Dish that Best Represents You or Your Business

Yu Sheng. It is a homegrown creation combining a mix of many ingredients and wonderful taste. People remember it fondly and keep coming back for more.

Company Culture

Cyclect is founded on hard work, innovation and a focus on excellence.

The company's heritage is marked by tumultuous events in history, riding several economic crises and political challenges. The pioneers of the company believed in family. Stakeholders like staff and customers are treated like family with a strong sense of trust and bond. Employees facing financial difficulty had always sought out the company to tide them through the toughest of times in the 60s and 70s. Even though the company had its own difficulties, the compassion and empathy of the founder, his sons and his grandsons still permeate the company today. Culturally, the company is a melting pot of many nationalities, from Europe to Asia, and yet they have one mind. Cyclect's motto "completely possible" expresses this mindset that the future is completely in their hands.

An Idiom to Describe Your Business
脚踏实地.

To step on solid ground. Cyclect works hard on fundamentals and proceeds to build their business in a stable and steady manner. Their purpose and values are fundamental to all their actions.

Ensure Engineering Pte Ltd

CEO Dr HAN Meng Siew

"You can never build one without passion, resilience, and above all, humility."

Company Profile

ENSURE is a one stop engineering service provider. It targets the infrastructural and process industries' operational and maintenance requirements by providing a concept of approach, developing relevant skill sets and providing support equipment to enhance or upkeep clients' facilities in optimum operational condition so that they can fulfil their obligations and achieve the purpose for which the facility is built.

Setbacks and Learning Points

Lack of "Unity of Purpose" in shareholders was the most memorable and disheartening experience in Dr Han's work life journey thus far, especially being a first-generation leader of the company. Although he understands that people may have different personal aspirations and it is their right to pursue them, of more importance to him was maintaining a passion for the company and wanting to be part of it.

Many lessons have been learnt from the handling of this issue, he says, and it has taught him of the need to develop a value system in the company's business culture, which will instil integrity.

As part of this, Ensure placed the need for fair returns for all stakeholders, including clients, staff and shareholders, into their system, whilst maintaining a strong emphasis on continuously improving their core competencies in a competitive and fast changing business environment.

In hindsight, the lessons learnt, although painful, were actually a blessing in disguise, he says. As they look into the future and succession planning, they can apply all the principles learnt to develop a conducive environment that encourages generations of future leaders to focus on the same cores values that have served the company well in the past.

Advice to Budding Entrepreneurs

Building an enterprise, first and foremost, is not about making money for better material enjoyment for yourself or your loved ones. In fact, it is quite the opposite. You have to sacrifice more than most to build one.

You can never build one without passion, resilience, and above all, humility. The need to learn and to learn quickly requires one to alter, rethink, and reshape one's own passionately devised plans, to twist or even change what was planned, which may be costly, at that point. Not willing to change will eventually cost you more than what was necessary.

Treasure good advice and be discerning of its intention, which is not easy for passionate entrepreneurs. Remember it is purposefulness that makes the difference in coming out with useful results and not speed. Once you have set your mind, purposefully pursue with all you have, which will assure you the best results you can ever hope to yield.

Failures are the best places to find answers for future successes. Do not let embarrassment, pride and disappointment lead you to miss out on these lessons, they are almost always relevant when you consider your next pursuit.

Finally, you need to be born with a little of an entrepreneurial nature, willing to venture into the unknown based on a reasonable evaluation of possibilities, and the rest is hard work for an extended period, not giving up the moral and spiritual aspirations that have served as a guide in what you will commit yourself to do. No success however impressive would be worth it if one loses his soul.

Must-have Qualities of Successful Entrepreneurs

- Determination, Focus and Soul
- Understand Self, Understand Stakeholders

Like all engineering service companies, Ensure could have easily gotten into self-preservation mode, busy doing what they know, trying out what they don't really know at the expense of others and stubbornly define who competitors are and try only to be better than them. In the Marine industry, and specifically repair works, which is a sunset industry, the best ones could last longer than others. Yet the eventual reality is that they will still go down as the industry goes down.

Thus, Ensure decided to diversify into well established, but growing industries where they could channel knowhow from the Marine into the Infrastructural and Process industries.

Getting into such well established industries was a huge challenge. The difference between what they knew and needed to know meant there was paradigm change that they needed to overcome. Yet Dr Han is not saying that the Marine industry does not produce "Quality" jobs, but rather, that the nature of the industry is different. When the ship has sailed off, your liability normally stops there. On the other hand, with Process Plants, your mistake would be remembered for years, which will affect your business. Therefore, the consciousness towards quality is more pronounced.

Hence, the need to not only innovate their system, but also upgrade the people became pressing. What they emerged with was an Integrated Management System that combines the needs of management for Quality, Safety, Health and Environmental considerations into a single service delivery package supported by Ensure's ERP system that provides a clear understanding. With concerted efforts to address their shortcomings, Ensure made progress and became more targeted in their approach in answering the challenges posed by clients.

With the service delivery designed to meet their challenges, clients began to respond and a business breakthrough was achieved. Having said that and looking back, Ensure is grateful for the opportunities clients have given them and today, say they are humbled and privileged to serve the largest company in the world in this business as a partner.

Significant Milestones

- The displacement of Shareholders as Directors of the company in 2001.
- Steps taken to develop a comprehensive management system, using information stored in a computer system to provide direction for business development from 2005 till date.
- Switching of business focus from Marine to Process industry.

The Next 50 Years

The advantage the company has is that its professionalism is always a welcoming aspect, says Dr Han. The region is presently the most dynamic economy in the world.

In the short term, Ensure needs to complete the fine tuning of its management model. In the medium term they need to foray into new markets to export their knowhow and management to establish companies around the region as a means of expansion.

In the long term, they need to continuously evolve to meet future demands and build a Management Culture that will be willing and capable of responding to challenges.

Dr Han hesitates to define what will happen in the next 50 years. Ensure has put up a reference for the company, that is "To be a World-Class Management Team" and so long as they stay focused on this Vision as a guiding principle, they can be confident of the future, he says.

The industry will also move towards renewable energy sources as the world runs out of options. At the same time, the growing need for energy is going to be more pressing as society becomes more affluent.

The other area would be water technology – purification and recycling of our water resources, for example.

These two sectors have huge room for development, including the necessary engineering services tailored for the industries.

Major Contributions to the Economy

- Managing environmental impact for a growing population and effluent management.
- Increasing competitiveness in the Process industry by having more reliable systems to operate on.
- Developing people, including intern students so that they may be challenged and thrive as they innovate themselves to be always relevant to meet the needs of society.

Representing Singapore Internationally

Ensure Engineering is a specialist engineering service provider serving the oil majors and MNCs in the petroleum and petrochemical industries in Singapore and the Asian region.

The economic growth and rapid infrastructure development in Asia offers tremendous potential for Ensure to represent Singapore on the international platform, says Dr Han.

Their specialised technology and innovation is recognised and endorsed by international oil majors and they have positioned themselves as the preferred partner in the regional markets of Asia.

Major Influence and Inspiration

Dr Han pays tribute to a simple man by the name of Mr Toh Kai Seng. Mr Toh is a retired professional engineer who had his own practice. He accepted Dr Han from the beginning into the company and personally made it his business to counsel him to be down to earth and to embrace integrity as a principle of business.

His mentoring guided Dr Han through many difficult episodes and is still a guiding light today. From Mr Toh's simple unassuming manner, Dr Han learnt to provide guidance to his staff on how they should perform their duties. Thankfully many followed and this is the single most important factor of Ensure's success thus far.

Mr Toh may not know he has influenced the way the company is run today, but Dr Han is grateful for his invaluable input; and now that he has retired and happily spending time with his grand-children, Dr Han wants to establish the same value system in the next generation.

Name a Local Dish that Best Represents You or Your Business

Singapore is a haven for good food but it does have its flip side and growing in age, this flip side has become more telling. For Dr Han, being a Hainanese growing up in an age where there was still abundance, particularly savours the Hainanese Mutton Soup, the way it was made in the earlier days. Dr Han thinks it epitomises the current state of his business. This delicacy is strong in flavour and character, meticulously blending meat and other ingredients, bringing out the best, aromatically soothing taste that is pleasing to the mouth.

Giving Back

Companies thrive on what the community needs and having benefited from the community, it is both a responsibility and obligation to give back to society.

For more than ten years, Ensure has within the company a working committee that looks into this aspect and one of the committee's objectives is to deliver returns to the community, especially in areas of education, social care and development.

Company Culture

To always conduct business and activities with Integrity, Professionalism and Responsibility.

An Idiom to Describe Your Business

"Know Yourself, Know Your Enemies, You Will Always Win"

EPChem International
Pte Ltd

CEO: SEAH Cheong Leng

"For a company to be able to continue in this business, they need a core team of dedicated staff who are passionate."

Company Profile

EPChem International Pte Ltd is a Singapore-based marketing and distribution company established in 1992. It supplies special performance chemicals in the Asia-Pacific region, focusing on wax and its related products and is widely regarded as the top GTL wax supplier and the most experienced FT wax supplier in the Asia Pacific region.

EPChem has a diverse and comprehensive product range which encompasses the entire series of hydrocarbon chain lengths in the form of wax and wax-like substances.

EPChem supplies to more than 30 countries across six continents and is constantly expanding market coverage and identifying new niche application areas.

Technical expertise by an in-house Wax Technology Department not only provides technical support to customers but is also constantly working to develop new in-house formulations using complementary products from its extensive product range.

Setbacks and Recovery

EPChem was the pioneer in identifying the use of vegetable wax as a replacement for paraffin wax in candle formulations. Business commenced in the year 2000 with the help and support of some government grants.

In 2006, a major palm oil company in a neighbouring country, but head-quartered in Singapore, approached EPChem to jointly collaborate on projects. Despite EPChem having its Technical Director, formulations and knowhow eventually being poached by this palm oil company, the company has moved on to develop new products and applications. All this has helped EPChem emerge a much stronger company.

Advice to Budding Entrepreneurs

- Be passionate about your business
- Be open-minded and look at all options
- Be honest and never overrate yourself
- Whenever you come up against an obstacle, step back and re-assess the situation by looking at the bigger picture before moving forward again

Must-have Qualities of Successful Entrepreneurs

- Be passionate about your business
- Persevere
- Always look forward to anticipate challenges ahead

Turning Point

It was in 2001 when EPChem decided to move away from a pure trading business to specialise in waxes and focus on niche application areas. This allowed them to develop their own EPIWAX brand which was widely recognised in the market.

Through their in-house technical support, EPChem was also able to build on their technical expertise allowing them to develop new application areas.

With this business model, EPChem has become an integral part of the supply chain for major wax producers who have found it more economical to tap onto EPChem's business network instead of working on their own. This is the reason why EPChem believes it is able to maintain a long-term relationship with partner principals and continues to add value to their business.

Significant Milestones

2001: When the business was redefined and EPChem started to focus on wax.

2009: When EPChem received their first Enterprise 50 award which gave them more exposure and confidence.

2014: When EPChem successfully secured the GTL hard wax distributorship from Shell MDS offering a much wider geographical coverage and significantly increased their volume. This has further enhanced the company's position as the region's most comprehensive wax supplier.

The Next 50 Years

EPChem is a knowledge-based company and succession has always been a major consideration — which is also the case with most SMEs.

All of EPChem's operations are fully automated, allowing them to capture knowledge and information into their two in-house and fully-customised systems — the Business Transaction System and the Multimedia Information Tracking System.

Singapore's labour market continues to remain tight; hence, the company is investing heavily in their HR department to ensure they continue to nurture key staff and attract the best talent.

Wax is a very interesting and dynamic business and ideally EPChem would like to look at opportunities with a bigger organisation with extensive regional infrastructure which will give them the chance to expand the business further.

The wax business is at a historical turning point. This is due to the exit of old technologies (Group I base oil) and the introduction of new substitutes. These substitutes come in the form of new natural products or new molecules created by new technologies.

The irony of this business is that it is probably too small for the big companies but too technically challenging for the smaller players.

For a company to be able to continue in this business, they need a core team of dedicated staff who are passionate about the business and able to continue to innovate and add value both to the principals as well as the customers.

Major Contributions to the Economy

More than 97% of business is outside Singapore; however EPChem

- works closely with universities and polytechnics – sharing our knowledge with them on special projects and providing internship opportunities, etc,
- has been running a profitable and transparent system with good, clean accounting records,
- sets aside funds annually to donate to charities via their investment company; Tigon Dynamics Pte Ltd.

Representing Singapore Internationally

EPChem operates in a very niche market and, throughout the years, they have been able to establish themselves as a key player in this industry. Despite EPChem's size, they have played a significant role and have had a resounding influence in the industry and its practices.

Similar to Singapore, EPChem has the ability to influence their stakeholders and has always been given the due respect despite their small size.

Major Influence and Inspiration

The late Mr Lee Kuan Yew was a major influence as he was a great political entrepreneur who built a country which offered very limited resources into a thriving metropolis admired by many.

In parallel, EPChem too started from humble beginnings in a country which had virtually no demand for wax! Often, it took years of development before seeing any tangible results materialise. Through sheer hard work and dedication, EPChem can now pride itself as being the top GTL wax supplier in the Asia Pacific.

Name a Local Dish that Best Represents You or Your Business

Durian. This "king of the fruits" is often regarded by many only by its generic name.

However, to durian lovers, this fruit has wide variations offering different tastes to cater to the demands of different people, different nationalities and to different palates.

Similarly, wax is often regarded by many as a commodity item. In fact, there is a wide spectrum of substances that fall under the definition of "wax". Interestingly, even new ones are being discovered from time to time!

Wax in itself is used by many in a surprisingly wide range of applications and this is often incomprehensible to many people.

Like durians, the price of wax can also range from a very low "give away price" to "top premium price", almost unmatched. The key to this business is the ability to match the right product to the right customer and hence derive the right price.

Giving Back

EPChem believes that money is made from the community. Therefore, it is only right to give back a portion of its earnings to the community. This is their little way of showing public-spiritedness and of being a good corporate citizen.

EPChem sets aside a five-digit donation annually to various organisations via their investment company. They continuously increase donations every year and, as far as possible, would like to ensure contributions go directly to the beneficiary.

Company Culture

EPChem say their company culture is modelled very much like a special force in the army. Staff are specialised in niche areas, fully exploiting IT technology to enhance their performance. They have a relatively small number of people covering a big geographical area and many different applications.

Company-wise, working as a team is important. There is a great trust placed on co-workers and a lot of the work done is on a very open and transparent basis.

In spirit, EPChem staff are passionate about their business and believe in a DIY culture. Computer systems, the website and brochures have all been designed internally.

An Idiom to Describe Your Business

"More than Just Wax".

At EPChem, they believe in establishing long-term relationships with their customers. They provide that added value to customers by sharing technical knowhow and market expertise with them.

They are also putting a strong emphasis on innovation so they continue to introduce new products and new applications in this dynamic market. They continue to discover new "wax-like" materials to introduce to customers and to grow the business with them.

"Long term wealth comes from doing the right thing and earning in the right way."

Company Profile

Singapore's leading precast concrete solutions provider, Excel Precast Pte Ltd was incorporated on 10 March 1999 to provide precast concrete design and manufacturing for the construction industry in Singapore. Excel Precast has a long and established reputation as an outstanding precast concrete solutions provider, consistently delivering high quality products on schedule via their superior logistics platforms. The company is committed to the highest level of teamwork and effective communication at all levels that provides clients with complete satisfaction and trust.

Excel Precast manufactures precast concrete products in its 17-hectare production facilities in Tampines (Singapore) and Johor (Malaysia). The production lines are outfitted with state-of-the-art equipment including three in-house Computerised Batching Plants (that comply with SS EN-206-1:2014 Standards), Prestressing Beds, Laboratory Facilities and Gantry Cranes. Excel Precast has diversified into multiple market sectors including HDB, private residential, industrial, commercial, learning institutions, military buildings and civil engineering projects.

Setbacks

There was one landmark project the company had been working very hard on where design and concept drawings had been produced. The client was initially convinced that this design was best suited for their project. However, Excel did not succeed in securing the project after the client visited the factory at Tuas. The reason? They were not confident that Excel were able to deliver the project to meet their expectations. Through this incident, CEO Mr Tan Bian Tiong realised the need for the company to be strong in all aspects. Strength in technical design alone was not sufficient if the company did not improve its image and quality of products. When the opportunity arose, they decided to shift their factory from Tuas to a bigger area in Tampines. This time, the production facility was set up to be more efficient and a strong emphasis was placed on the quality of products produced. This led to the fast expansion of Excel's market volume and gave them a strong reputation.

Advice to Budding Entrepreneurs

Even the stream of water will win against the hard river stone with persistency.

Must-have Qualities of Successful Entrepreneurs

- Long term wealth comes from doing the right thing and earning in the right way.
- We are human beings, soft outside and strong inside; and not like a crab that is strong outside and soft inside and has difficulty in interacting with other people.
- Open-minded, forward-looking approach, constant flow of ideas and be practical.

Turning Point

The winning of one of the HDB projects located at Punggol East in the year 2008, which consisted of 500 units of apartments with a multi-storey car park.

This project was not only large to Excel then but also triggered production capacity that went beyond Singapore.

Significant Milestones

Stage 1 (1999 – 2007) — Exploration & establishment of market.

Stage 2 (2008 – 2013) — Expansion and fast growth.

Stage 3 (2014 onwards) — Adopt latest modular construction technology for further expansion.

The Future

For the next 20 years:

- Expand the business beyond Singapore
- Innovate amd expand in a new field of business.

Industry Trends in the Next 50 Years

For the next few decades, the industry in Singapore will start to adopt a less labour-dependent method of construction. Appropriate business ventures will also be explored in other countries.

Major Contributions to the Economy

- Create job vacancies
- Boost the construction industry
- Help to fulfil the demand in housing
- Spin-off demand in transportation industry

Representing Singapore Internationally

- High and consistent product quality
- Fast and reliable construction system
- Innovative and environmentally-friendly

Major Influence and Inspiration

"The task of the leaders must be to provide or create for them a strong framework within which they can learn, work hard, be productive and be rewarded accordingly." - Lee Kuan Yew.

Name a Local Dish that Best Represents You or Your Business

Laksa. To Excel, laksa embodies the willingness to innovate and try new things.

Giving Back

Excel believes in giving back to society and nurturing the younger generation through better education. In this regard, they support the Children's Society, NUS and NTU.

Company Culture

The organisation believes in work-life balance & cohesion as part of the company culture. Employees have close relations, trust and work co-operatively to be their best.

An Idiom to Describe Your Business

The company's Core Values can be explained in three words.
Explore. Exceed. Excel

Explore: Technologies, Ideas, Perspectives, Boundaries and Paradigms
Exceed: Customer Expectations, Limitations, Capabilities, Performance
Excel: Quality, Service, Innovation, Creativity and Spirit

Feinmetall Singapore Pte Ltd

General Manager, SAM Chee Wah

"A successful leader needs to have an open mind
— not for complimentary flowery words
but rather criticism."

Company Profile

Feinmetall Singapore Pte Ltd (Feinmetall Singapore) was officially incorporated in March 2007. Initially, it only had a small team of five people and its business came mainly from supporting customers who used Feinmetall products. Today, Feinmetall Singapore has a staff strength of forty five and has moved up the value chain to become a one-stop design, manufacturing, testing and service provider for wafer probe cards, utilising cutting-edge technology from Germany.

Feinmetall Singapore is best known for its strong technical capabilities, its good mix of product and service offerings, and its excellent reputation in the industry. Feinmetall has in fact become so successful that it has invested in its new facilities to expand its production capacity, and its vision for the long term is "to be recognised as the most respectable probe card solution provider in South East Asia".

Setbacks and Recovery

Back in 2009 when the financial crisis struck, Feinmetall experienced a sharp fall of orders. Customers were either having short work weeks or their plants shut down. Their production floors had either partially or totally turned their lights off in broad daylight. The factory was only operating three days per week with no visibility of orders.

Tension was high and many competitors were also cutting back. But Feinmetall continued to pursue regular visits to customers, not so much to discuss business but rather to comfort them on the current situation. During this period, they established an in-depth relationship with many customers by understanding their needs and expectations. When the financial crisis turned around, their well maintained probe cards prepared customers for their production ramp-up in 2010. Feinmetall also hit its record revenue and net income in 2010. The revenue record of 2010 was not broken until 2013, while the net income record still remains unbroken. The lesson learnt was never give up on your customers in bad times and they will not give up on you when good times comes.

Advice to Budding Entrepreneurs

The entrepreneurial journey is challenging and lonely. When you embark on this journey, you have to be prepared to:

- Give it your best to shape the company for the future
  Only if you are committed to give your best effort to build a business, can obstacles be overcome. You pick yourself up, swallow your pride and move on gracefully.

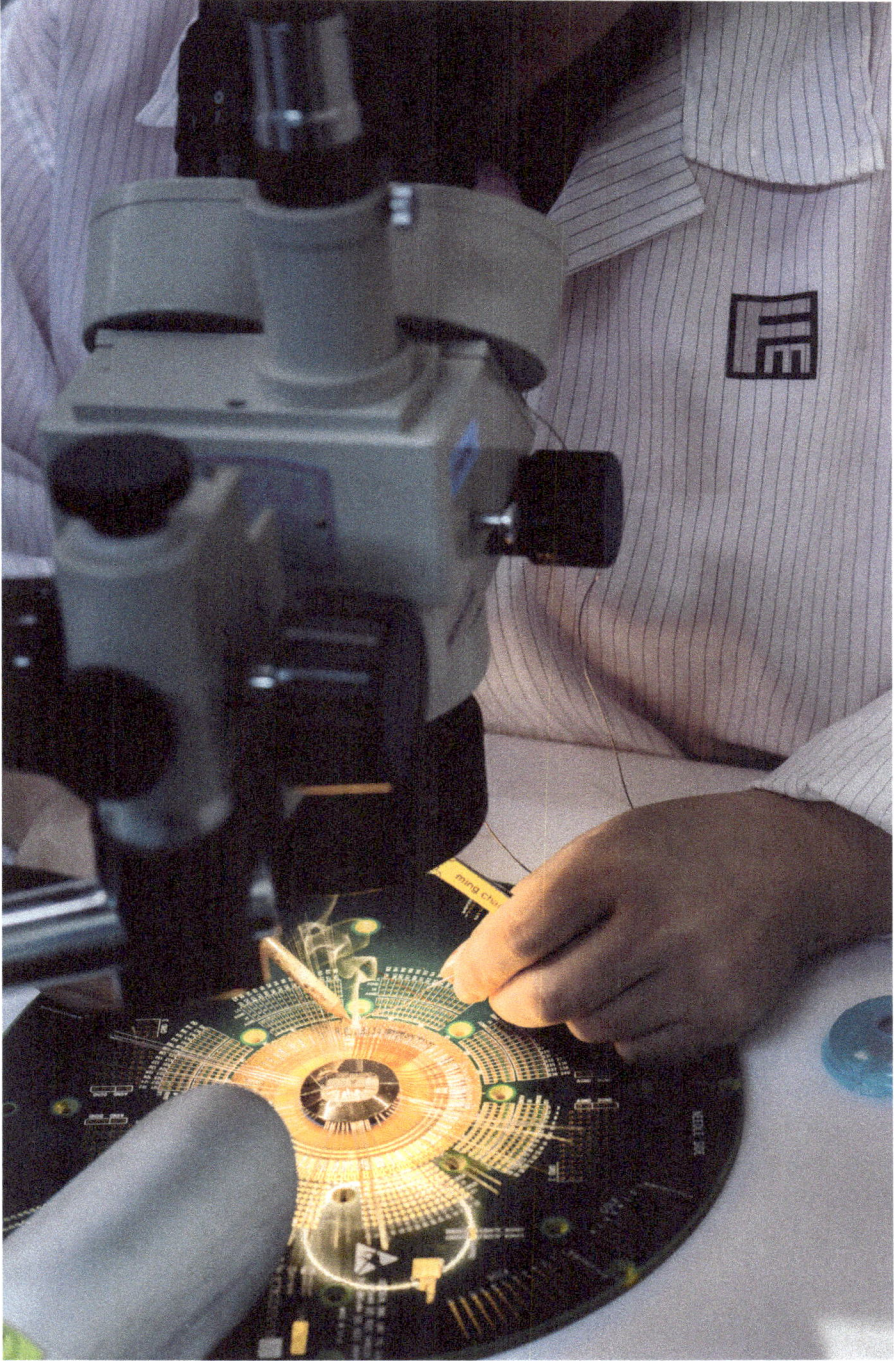

- Lead and nurture a team that believes in your vision
  Only like-minded people can come together with mutual trust and courage. A leader is never able to lead unless he has a team that believes in him and his vision to bring the company to where they want it to be.

- Seize every opportunity
  Opportunities may appear in many forms, but only the well-prepared seize them. Be humble to ask, be stupid to assume but be bold to take on the challenge.

Must-have Qualities of Successful Entrepreneurs

- Open-mindedness: A successful leader needs to have an open mind — not for complimentary flowery words, but rather for criticism of what you have not done right. Only with an open mind, can you understand, analyse, accept, adapt to the business environment and formulate strategies to steer your business onto the right path.

- A big heart: Entrepreneurs need to have a big heart for their stakeholders and the community. While profitability is the key survival factor, it is not the only objective of business. Understanding and fulfilling customer requirements, accommodating supplier concerns, caring for your employees' well-being and giving back to the community are the other aspects of being a successful entrepreneur.

- Integrity: This is the most important quality of a successful entrepreneur. As a leader, you need to uphold integrity to do right by your stakeholder. Integrity shapes the honesty, righteousness and values of your business. Honour your commitment to customers, suppliers, employees and investors as a personal and company value.

Turning Point

In 2013, Feinmetall had the opportunity to provide their local manufacturing services to some reputable customers in Europe. The team pulled together and produced a high quality finished product. They won the contract to be the only manufacturing site to supply cantilever probe cards to European customers. Since then, sales revenue has increased by 20% year-on-year. With this platform, they continue to expand the business to other parts of the world.

Significant Milestones

In 2008, they developed the local manufacturing capability of Cantilever Probe

Card. This capability helped them to open doors to many customers as the entry barrier is relatively low. They grew their customer base with this capability.

In 2011, Feinmetall transferred the manufacturing of entry-level vertical probe card processes from Germany to Singapore. This milestone has given them a competitive advantage to offer short lead time, lower price and local support to entry-level vertical probe cards. They also increased market penetration with this capability.

In 2014, they simplified their cantilever card production processes and automated many manufacturing instructions. This improvement helped increase their capacity, productivity and lead time and hence, increased revenue by 20%.

The Next 50 Years

In the next 50 years, semiconductor testing may have become simplified to the point that wafer probing may be done without any hardware. Testing may be in the form of laser, verifying the wafer reliability through contactless testing. Test data may be visible through the web and the business could be providing knowledge-based training, software and applications instead of supplying of hardware.

Moving forward, semiconductor testing may still be focused on fine pitch, small bond pad and high temperature resistance. Social media and apps could be the main platform to drive semiconductor sales. Blue-tooth, wireless and mobile hardware will continue to migrate to a different platform in application software rather than hardware. The Internet will continue to connect the world globally without borders.

Major Contributions to the Economy

Feinmetall is committed to continuous technology upgrading and hence, able to bring forward many testing solutions that enable product designers to introduce more multi-functional devices to the world.

Feinmetall's local manufacturing facility is committed to grow its R&D and advanced manufacturing capability. This commitment

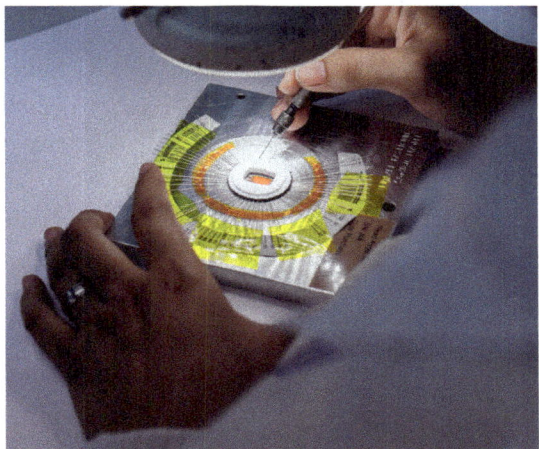

will continue to drive more employment for PMETs into the semiconductor sector.

They are one of the rare players in the wafer test supply chain in Singapore. With the commitment to expansion in Singapore, they believe they can support many multinational semiconductor companies wanting to establish a foothold in Singapore.

Representing Singapore Internationally

Feinmetall has established a reputable brand image in Singapore and abroad. Feinmetall has its own technology platform and will continue to expand to provide probing solutions in the ever changing semiconductor testing arena. With a commitment to expand in this region, they are confident they can represent Singapore on an international platform.

Major Influence and Inspiration

Mr Sam considers his late mother, Mdm Chan Kam Hah his biggest inspiration. While she was born into a family that could not afford her an education, she learnt to read herself. While she was only a simple housewife till the age of 39, she upheld her integrity, and that shaped him since young. When she joined the workforce, she took pride in her job and gave back to community within her means. His major influence is her determination towards life. She never gave up hope despite the adverse environment, and maintained her commitment towards life-long learning, family, work and the community. She inspired Mr Sam to be honest and to uphold integrity. She believes if we lose these values and win the world, we lose ourselves; and that, is everything.

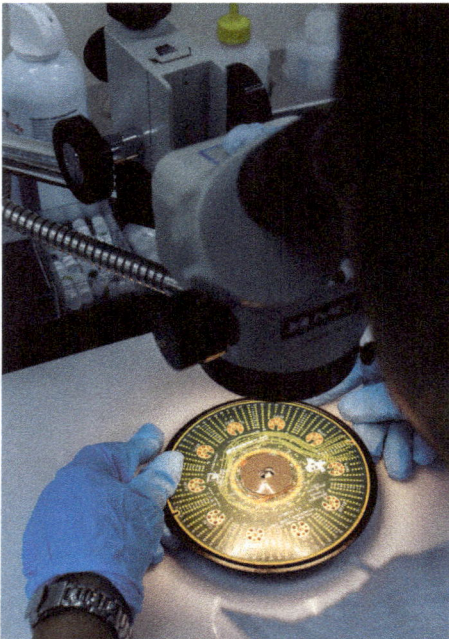

Name a Local Dish that Best Represents You or Your Business

Laksa, a popular Peranakan spicy noodle soup which is a combination of Chinese and Malay cuisine. While the rice noodle is plain and tasteless, the secret laksa gravy makes the dish irresistible. The ingredients are commonly known to anyone but how you formulate it to beat your competitors, standing above them, reflects dynamic strategies and passion for the business. The spicy taste symbolises courage to meet the day-to-day challenges without fear.

Giving Back

The company values integrity, care and team spirit. They truly believe giving back to community is an excellent means to bond and show employees how to contribute their fair share to the community.

Company Culture

Openess and Trust. The company works in an open culture whereby the management has regular communication sessions with the staff on business performance, new announcements and also to gather feedback for improvement. Employees are also encouraged to put up their suggestions for both official and recreational activities. The company operates with a high level of trust between the management and staff. This is important to the success of the business and the staff are self-motivated with less supervision to perform.

An Idiom to Describe Your Business

Never give an excuse for your failure but always find a reason for your success.

Franklin Offshore Holdings Pte Ltd

CEO Angie TANG

*"Be prepared for the long haul and persevere.
Work hard but smart too."*

Company Profile

In 1985, Franklin Offshore began operations in Singapore and was initially focused on the provision of steel wire rope and other rigging equipment. The business grew and in 1997, they expanded their scope of business to the provision of mooring equipment and services.

Today, the Franklin Offshore Group of Companies is a leading integrated provider of quality steel wire rope, rigging and mooring equipment and services, serving the marine oil and gas and offshore construction industry. Their expertise includes the manufacture of cable-laid slings and Flemish-Lock® slings and the provision of inspection and load testing services. They also provide high-quality integrated solutions in temporary and permanent mooring projects including a range of offshore installation construction services.

The Group, which is headquartered in Singapore, has, over the years, expanded its global business footprint beyond Singapore to cover Australia, Indonesia, South Korea, Azerbaijan, Qatar, the United States of America and the Netherlands.

Setbacks

Like most heavy industries, the offshore oil and gas industry is male dominated and rugged. It is not a typical industry that a woman would find affinity with. Fortunately, Ms Tang had been exposed to the heavy industry as soon as she joined the workforce and has learnt the ropes of the trade over the years.

The major players in the international offshore oil and gas market are mainly from the West and Franklin Offshore being Asian had to work very hard in the early days to establish and prove themselves to be a credible supplier of quality equipment and services. Over time, Franklin has developed a proven track record that has propelled our business beyond the shores of Singapore.

Franklin also relied very much on the support of banks for credit facilities to finance their business expansion. Today, they have established credit worthiness amongst the banks but it was not easy in the early days when the company was still in the infancy stage and lacked a proven track record in the market. This has no doubt helped to grow the business to what it is today.

Offshore oil and gas specialists are rare talents within the region and even worldwide. Very often, one has to source for such talents all over as they are always in high demand in the industry.

As Franklin expand geographically, they face challenges in doing business in different cultures and business environments. They have a presence in Asia,

Australia, America, Europe and the Middle East and have to learn to manage the workforce and deal with customers across various cultures.

It is definitely not easy building up Franklin Offshore but it is not impossible, either. Ms Tang and her team learnt to persevere and work hard to prove themselves to the market. To gain customers' and bankers' confidence, this cannot be done overnight. Time and effort are needed. One must also be willing to learn and adapt, especially when dealing with different cultures.

Advice to Budding Entrepreneurs

Be prepared for the long haul and persevere. Work hard but smart too. Be connected to the market and learn from successful entrepreneurs on how to be a great leader.

The hardship Ms Angie Tang says she has gone through in the early days of the business has moulded her into a resilient person. Perseverance and hard work, coupled with humility has contributed to her success today.

Do not be afraid or embarrassed to seek assistance when you need it. Learn as much as possible when opportunity knocks, internalise it and apply it to your business.

Must-have Qualities of Successful Entrepreneurs
* Resilience
* Humble, hardworking and willing to learn
* Able to take calculated risks

Turning Point

The company started small and hence the management style in the early days was an informal one and there was no need for a formalised structure. When they grew to a certain size, Franklin felt they needed a more formalised corporate structure to support further growth. In 2007, 3i and ICG invested in Franklin Offshore and they helped to run the business more professionally. In 2013, the Management decided to embark on a management buyout exercise to buy back all the shares from the external shareholders as they felt that they were ready and in a position to lead Franklin Offshore to the next phase of growth on their own.

Significant Milestones in Developing Your Business

1997: started providing temporary mooring services and solutions

2008: started providing permanent mooring services and solutions

2009: established European operations in the Netherlands which today has the largest waterfront facility (in the Port of Rotterdam) within the Franklin Offshore Group

The Next 50 Years

Franklin sees itself gaining a stronger foothold in the European market through a wholly owned subsidiary in the Netherlands where the Group's largest facility is situated, specifically, in the Port of Rotterdam. Comprising an area of over 70,000m² and a 228m long quay, the waterfront facility holds much potential for business growth and development.

They will continue to anchor the business in rigging and mooring which is their core competence. The company is on the lookout for possible merger and acquisition targets which can synergise with existing operations. They may also explore higher-valued added business activities that complement the existing scope of business.

Industry Trends in The Next 50 Years

Ms Tang is hesitant to foresee the trends or comment about the industry development in the next 50 years. She only says that the oil and gas industry will continue to exist but

companies must be able to ride through the cyclical downturn. Effective cost management and maintaining healthy cash flow is the way to move forward regardless of which industry you are in.

Major Contributions to the Economy

Being a major local player in the rigging and mooring market, they have contributed to the oil and gas sector internationally.

Franklin provides employment to about 220 Singapore citizens and permanent residents and about 430 other nationalities worldwide.

They promote the Singapore brand as Franklin Offshore is founded and headquartered in Singapore.

Representing Singapore Internationally

Franklin Offshore has flown the Singapore flag internationally in the countries where they have established operations. They supply rigging equipment (e.g. cable-laid slings and Flemish-Lock® slings) for use in offshore oilfields and they also execute mooring projects in offshore oilfields which are all located outside Singapore. Hence, they have brought made-in-Singapore products and services into the international oil and gas sector.

Major Influence and Inspiration

When Ms Tang was young, it was her mother who inspired her, not because she was successful financially, but because she was successful in overcoming all the difficulties in life to bring up five children alone when her father passed away when she was just six years old.

As young Angie grew up and started her career, she was lucky to have met a few good mentors who have guided her and gave her the opportunity to learn and improve herself in business. One whom she will always appreciate is her present Chairman Mr Peter Lew. He has taught and guided her and gave her the motivation to be what she is today.

When the business became successful, she was further influenced and inspired by some community leaders and mentors to expand her networking circle. Besides that, she also started to learn more about Corporate Social Responsibility. The company has contributed much back to society to assist the needy not only in monetary terms but also in kind e.g. Staff Volunteers.

Name a Local Dish that Best Represents You or Your Business

Chilli Crab best represents the business — and the majority of Franklin's customers love Chilli Crab!

Giving Back

As corporate citizens, Ms Tang believes companies should fulfil their fair share of responsibilities towards society by giving back.

The company's primary CSR focus is on needy children. They also wish to inculcate a strong sense of CSR amongst staff. Hence, they do not just contribute financially but also put in time and effort. They encourage staff members to be involved personally in the various CSR activities and have first-hand experience in helping and sharing. The aim is to mould Franklin Offshore into a successful business with a heart.

Company Culture

Franklin Offshore is like a close-knit family, says Ms Tang. The management style in the early days was an informal one as the company was small and did not need a structured corporate style. This helped to forge a close, personal and strong relationship between management and staff and has contributed to the strong staff retention capability of the company.

The size of the company has grown over the years and the Group's staff strength numbers about 650 worldwide currently. For effective management and control of the larger Group, the management style has evolved to a more corporate one whereby roles, responsibilities and functions are more clearly defined and accounted for. The company has, at the same time, retained the personal touch and closeness to the rank and file which is a very important contributing factor to the stability of the business.

An Idiom to Describe Your Business

The sky's the limit!

Gain City Best-Electric Pte Ltd

CEO: Danny TEO

"Be sincere and trustworthy in everything he does, and maintain a continual pursuit of perfection."

Company Profile

Gain City aims to build a long-term relationship with customers by providing them with the best shopping experience each time they visit a Gain City store. Equipped with integrity and professionalism, they are committed to carry out their vision diligently, offering value-added products and services to customers, while scaling new heights in business.

CEO Mr Teo lets on that 4 core values summarise the business and guide the way it is run.

- Trustworthiness
- Professionalism
- Business Ethics
- Excellence

Setbacks

When Mr Teo first started out in 1981, the new Government policy (then) of the relocation of land (1981 土地搬迁) created much difficulty. From this experience he learnt that in order to succeed, an indomitable attitude is very important.

Advice to Budding Entrepreneurs

- Be trustworthy, both to customers and business partners
- Have enough determination
- Always try to attain mutually beneficial (互惠互利) outcomes with customers/ business partners

Must-have Qualities of Successful Entrepreneurs

- Trustworthiness
- Determination
- Knowledge of how to attain mutually beneficial outcomes (互惠互利) with customers / business partners

Turning Point

Every economic recession was a turning point for Gain City.

Significant Milestones

1983: Setting up of first shop in Towner Road
2013: Setting up at AMK HQ
2015: Sungei Kadut Building

The Next 50 Years

Mr Teo foresees the business growing and gaining recognition regionally, becoming a major regional retailer. The Consumer Electronics industry is generally getting bigger, while land space is getting more and more expensive, meaning rents have risen substantially. As a result, it's a seen trend that as more CE retailers shrink in size due to the high rents, Gain is getting their own land and building so as to be a one-stop shop with a full product range that enables customers to enjoy the visual and physical touch of the actual products. In time, he added, this will make Gain stand out from the competition to give the maximum returns to customers and also outshine competitors.

Major Contributions to the Society/Economy

- Gain's aim from the start was to be the first choice consumer electronics retailer with a mission to beautify consumers' homes.
- Over the years, Gain has trained scores of technicians and helped to improve the lot of this set of workers through a Variable Bonus system. Under this scheme, not only can technicians be the boss of their own project, they are also well-protected by company policy and insurance.
- The introduction and perfection of Gain's Service Connections system has pushed up the overall service standard and expectations in the industry. Consumers can now expect higher standards and services from retailers.

Major Influence and Inspiration

Mr Teo cites his parents. They taught him to be sincere and trustworthy in everything he does, and to continually pursue perfection. Their example has made him the person he is and this is reflected in the way his business is run.

Name a Local Dish that Best Represents You or Your Business

Fruit Salad. The business consists of many different brands, and Gain has workers of many different races. Yet, everyone comes together to create a sizzling sensation just like a bowl of fruit salad, which is a healthy mix of food with splendid flavouring.

Giving Back

Just like the old Chinese proverb, "Predecessors plant the trees, so that the descendants can have cool cover", Singapore's pioneers have given us what we have now to safeguard for the next generations. Mr Teo says he wants to follow in their

footsteps and give back whenever possible. That's why he is involved in charity to help out those in need.

Company Culture

Gain is still a very traditional company which believes in hard work and endurance. Mr Teo has trained staff to not be afraid of difficulties and to believe in their capabilities and always strive for the best. He has a goal to make Gain City the first-choice employer when it comes to where to work at, just like how he aims to make Gain City the top retailer in the minds of consumers.

An Idiom to Describe Your Business

Excellence (精益求精), says Mr Teo. He says he has very high expectations of everything and everyone, including himself and the business. He believes that only when we strive for excellence, can we achieve even more excellence and perfection, and only then will there be improvements and breakthroughs.

Golden Bridge Foods Manufacturing Pte Ltd

MD: ONG Bee Chip

"It is important to set start and end dates. Each milestone must have a start and end date."

Company Profile

Set up in 1993, Golden Bridge Foods Manufacturing Pte Ltd has been thriving in the processed food industry for more than 20 years. Today, they have become a successful household name in the processed food industry in Singapore and in Asia. With a bold vision to be a leading international food company, they continue to innovate to offer clients superior food solutions, now and in the future. As Singapore's leading one-stop manufacturer and supplier of processed meats to retailers, wholesale food distributors and foodservice companies, the company prides itself on its ability to fulfil their varied needs. Beyond Singapore, their products can be found in major supermarket chains as well as hotels, restaurants and cafes across 15 countries.

Memorable Setback and Lessons Learnt

In 2013, due to a fire caused by faulty electrical outlets, 40% of their production area and machines were damaged. During that period, production lines were down and they could not fulfil customer orders.

The main concern then was to resume production as soon as possible.

However, most of the machines had to be purchased from Europe. Within six months they managed to purchase the machines required and started production.

From these six months, Mr Ong believes one of the most important things he has learnt is perseverance. One should not give up when the going gets tough. He first identified the issues that caused the faulty electrical outlets and henceforth, strengthened the fire alarm systems. He also ensured a system of regular maintenance of the electrical outlets in the company.

Advice to Budding Entrepreneurs

Being a successful entrepreneur often encompasses a series of mistakes before finally nailing the right idea or business. There are actually no shortcuts in starting a business. It is acceptable to clarify any doubts in mind.

Must-have Qualities of Successful Entrepreneurs

- Attitude: The right attitude and relentless passion to solve problems. Do not expect to always succeed. All new businesses encounter tough times. Successful entrepreneurs need the passion to get through those times without giving up.
- Perseverance: With every step, entrepreneurs get closer to achieving their definitive objective or vision. However, not all steps are easy. Successful

entrepreneurs will only make it past the difficult times by persevering.

- Creativity: One facet of creativity is being able to make connections between seemingly unrelated events or situations.

Turning Point

Golden Bridge realised that to grow bigger, they would have to export. Only with increased export sales, can they achieve economies of scale and spread costs over a larger volume of revenue. Also, exporting minimises the effect of seasonal fluctuations in sales and helps achieve a stable sales pattern. This increases the sales potential for products and reduces risk. Shelf life plays a vital role in exporting products. This is why they started manufacturing canned luncheon meat and a portion pack series. Currently, Golden Bridge exports to more than 15 countries.

Significant Milestones

It is firstly important to identify crucial business-plan goals. Mr Ong has set short- and long-term goals for the business. His goals focus on profits, marketing, brand recognition and community outreach. Mr Ong believes we have to always remove unrealistic goals from the list, as they do not contribute to the milestones. So, communication with different key personnel is important.

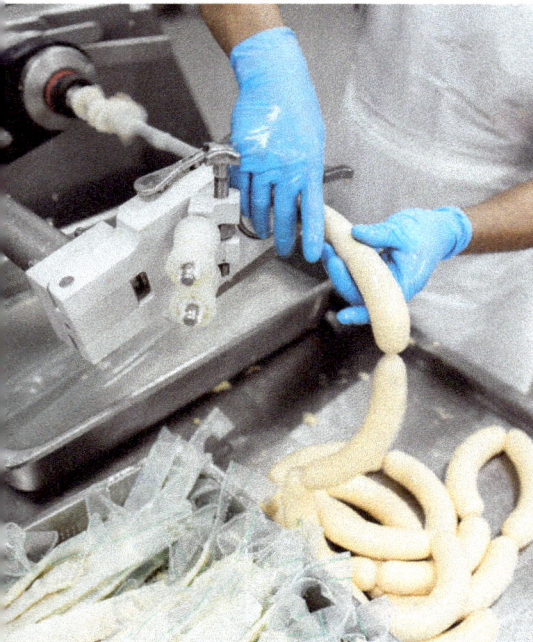

He forms a team to fulfil the goals set. He often encourages his employees to work independently so that they have plenty of chances to learn.

Each milestone Mr Ong sets requires a project timeline and a budget. This is so that employees understand the resources with which they have to reach the milestone.

The Next 50 Years

Golden Bridge is now the leading processed meat supplier in Singapore. As the next step, they are preparing for an IPO in the next few years. In 50 years, they see themselves being the largest processed meat supplier in Asia.

In the next 50 years, Mr Ong perceives meat processing to be done in countries with raw material supplies, yet still upholding Singapore's strict requirements. At present, 85% of Golden Bridge's supplies are mostly from Canada, Brazil and Denmark. Golden Bridge will continue to be headquartered in Singapore, where research and development will be carried out. This will in turn reduce overall manufacturing costs and increase profitability.

Contributions to the Economy

Singapore is a small country with no natural resources. In the past, people reasoned that Singapore firms are only capable of importing products from other countries. However, many companies, including Golden Bridge, have proven that they are also able to export to other countries around the world. Golden Bridge is proud to be the first canned meat manufacturer in Singapore.

Representing Singapore Internationally

Golden Bridge manufactures premium products in Singapore which comply with safety requirements set by the government to inspire confidence among customers. Golden Bridge has attained Enterprise 50; an award only given to the top 50 SMEs in Singapore as well as FSSC 22000, a food safety certification recognised globally. On the international platform, Golden Bridge showcases itself as a superior brand with safe and flavoursome products.

Major Influence and Inspiration

Mr Ong cites his father who was a successful businessman in many industries. Although his father had only three months of formal schooling, he was a wise and far-sighted man. He always made the right decisions. His never-give-up spirit has truly inspired Mr Ong. He had endured the hardship of World War II. When the war ended in 1945, his father started to work as a delivery assistant to help out the family. He also pushed himself to obtain a driving license upon reaching the legal age, in order to be promoted to the senior position of lorry driver. Despite the meagre pay as he started his career, he learnt and formed his own business principles and philosophies, which later proved to beneficial in the success of his own business ventures in the years to come.

He was not afraid of failures. One of his businesses was related to textile printing. He knew that in order to expand it, hands-on printing had to be eliminated and automation was crucial. He was the first businessman in Singapore to introduce textile printing machines from Holland. With his ideas, he approached the banks and got approval for the loans required to purchase the machines. Back in the days, getting a loan from the bank was an almost unachievable task unless the banks saw that the project was close to 100% feasible.

His father is a man who exemplified that with diligence, passion and clear vision, one can build a successful business. He grew his business as a young man without any capital, and believed that with good reputation and hard work, one will achieve success. Since young, he often instillled in his children that with success and fortune, one must give back to society and help the less fortunate.

Name a Local Dish that Best Represents You or Your Business

Yam Ring.

Yam Ring symbolises "Togetherness" as it is round in shape. It is also often associated with unity, wholeness and infinity. Working in Golden Bridge makes employees feel like they are all a big family. Mr Ong treats his employees like his family and customers like his friends. It is important to treat all employees with care and respect as he truly believes that great customer service begins with great employee relations.

Giving Back

Giving back to the community is very important. Being successful comes with a great responsibility to provide for others. Every quarter, Mr Ong donates to various communities locally and internationally for people in need. Influenced by his father, he strongly believes that being successful comes with the responsibility of giving back to people who truly need the help.

Company Culture

Golden Bridge adopts a family-style business culture. Through the years, Mr Ong realises that employees need to feel a sense of belonging in order to find meaning in their work. This is why creating a family atmosphere is beneficial. A family corporate culture will also help information to flow smoothly from the highest tiers to the lowest. Such a corporate culture will breed loyalty and it will inspire staff members to do their best.

An Idiom to Describe Your Business

Think out of the box. Thinking outside the box means to think differently, unconventionally, or from a new perspective. It is important to approach problems in new, innovative ways; conceptualising problems differently. Golden Bridge constantly keeps up with the pace to stay ahead of the competition.

Greenpac (S) Pte Ltd

CEO: Susan CHONG

"Embarking on a green business journey does not necessarily mean a compromise on the bottom line."

Company Profile

Established in 2002, Greenpac is a knowledge-based company which helps customers to design, develop and re-engineer innovative, environmentally friendly and holistic packaging solutions that achieve bottom-line cost savings.

Over the years, Greenpac has also forged strategic partnerships with market leaders who manufacture unique environmentally friendly packaging materials by being the sole distributor for their products in the Asia Pacific region. In tandem with the growing needs of customers, Greenpac has also expanded its core business activities to include new services such as Heat Treatment, Kit Packaging, Programme Management, Logistics Services, and Professional Packaging Services.

Setbacks and Lessons Learnt

More than ten years ago, environmentally friendly packaging was still rarely adopted in most parts of Southeast Asia, including Singapore, as most customers equate environmental packaging to higher costs. People often have the misconception that being green is expensive. It took lots of hard work and persistence to convince and educate customers that green packaging actually leads to an overall cost reduction, on top of greening the supply chain. Therefore, before Greenpac could start supplying eco-friendly packaging, it had to create demand.

Educating customers on the importance of going green, breaking old mindsets that using eco-friendly materials was costly, and getting customers' buy-in to re-engineer their current packaging processes were some of the business challenges Greenpac had to overcome. In the early days, they had to educate customers about the benefits they can derive from re-analysing their packaging processes.

Greenpac then shifted focus from simply supplying eco-friendly packaging to finding cost efficiencies in the packaging design by using eco-friendly materials. Thus, re-engineering the packaging design to minimise consumption of materials and wastage of space, without compromising the functionality and performance of the packaging, became an integral part of its business model.

Advice to Budding Entrepreneurs

As a budding entrepreneur particularly aiming for a breakthrough innovation, you need to change the game plan. Innovation is not just about adding value in a superficial manner, or adding more of the same. That would be like providing the same thing at a lower cost, creating better, yet similar products, or giving better but the same service. It is more about adding value incrementally, which is good for a

company that is striving for continuous improvement.

For a business to be a game-changer, you need to fundamentally shift the way things are done through innovation.

You need to change the game.

You need to question the traditional and conventional methods of doing things. At times, you may even have to move away from long-accepted rules to lay the ground for new ones.

That is where the breakthrough in innovation comes about.

For budding lady entrepreneurs in a male-dominated industry, it means that you have to sometimes work harder than your competitors to earn respect. You have to lead by example.

Must-have Qualities of Successful Entrepreneurs

- Be sincere with trusted working partners and keep good relationships. Today, packaging is all about customising solutions to each customer's specific needs. In Greenpac, leveraging on environmentally friendly packaging solutions and working with trusted partners, they are able to offer customers a total packaging solution that results in significant costs savings.
- Constantly upgrade and be a relevant leader. In order to lead a company that constantly seeks out and equips itself with the latest knowhow, a leader must also invest in herself/himself too by attending well-recognised leadership development programmes.
- Greenpac succeeds because everyone, including Greenpac's staff, business partners, family and clients, share a common aim and vision. They are all

committed to building a sustainable future today. If they keep true to this, they will continue to be successful. Therefore, a successful leader must drive this and to work towards achieving the common goal.

Significant Milestones

2008: Enterprise 50 Award (in 4th place) awarded by KPMG and Business Times
2012: Shifting into new 200,000 sq ft Green Factory at Boon Lay
2014: Singapore Quality Awards
2014: Ernst & Young Entrepreneur of the Year

The Next 50 Years

Success is a journey and not a destination. Ms Chong envisions Greenpac becoming a world-class knowledge-based company with a global brand that stands for total and innovative environmentally-friendly packaging solutions. She aims to realise this vision through continuous innovation, research and development.

Ms Chong believes that cost-effective "green" packaging is the way of the future. Embarking on a green business journey does not necessarily mean a compromise on the bottom line. On the contrary, it makes sense to go into a green business now. Packaging which is sustainable and can be reused many times helps to cut down on material cost and production cost. Also, they re-engineer existing packaging and cut down on unnecessary materials. The eventual packaging is lighter and helps the customer save significantly on freight cost.

Globally, more and more companies, especially multinational corporations, are starting to 'green' their operations now and in future. It is an opportunity to offer green solutions and services to these companies.

Representing Singapore Internationally

Winning the EY Entrepreneur of the Year for Sustainable Packaging Solutions in 2014 was a kind of affirmation that Greenpac are doing the right thing. The award will definitely encourage them to keep pursuing sustainable methods in providing packaging solutions to customers, which is not an easy task.

The company's constant strive for excellence has also caught the attention of the business community and Greenpac has achieved a string of prestigious business awards in Singapore and internationally.

Just to name a few, Greenpac is one of the winners of the WorldStar Packaging Award every year since 2009. These prestigious awards are awarded by the World Packaging Organisation (WPO). WPO is located in USA. It is a non-profit, non-

governmental, international federation of national packaging institutes and associations, regional packaging federations and other interested parties including corporations and trade associations.

Major Influence and Inspiration

All the drive and motivation in her life are not borne from nothing, says Ms Chong. Coming from an entrepreneurial family, her mother in Kedah, Malaysia, is her source of inspiration. Her mother did not have an education, spending most of her time learning how to cook and create flower arrangements, though she did not live the life of a tai-tai. This lasted until Ms Chong was 10 years old, when her father's business went bust during the financial crisis, forcing her mother to start working. She joint ventures with a publisher to sell and distribute kindergarten books in the northern part of Malaysia. A lot of hard work was put in, and she persisted despite the harsh environment. Ms Chong really admires the transformation of her mother from a housewife who knew nothing about business, into a very well-respected business person.

Name a Local Dish that Best Represents You or Your Business

Customisation of a packaging is a lot like cooking. Ms Chong enjoys keeping herself busy in the kitchen, where instinct and inventiveness count. By not following a recipe, recreating a taste requires some precision but, more importantly; it is about intuition and creativity.

A wrap (or popiah) will not be just a flour-wrap if you are creative with the fillings. It can be created and customised to suit the local taste or more sophisticated to suit international preferences.

Giving Back

Greenpac views corporate social responsibility (CSR) as part of corporate sustainability. Greenpac's business was conceptualised around CSR and focused on three key thrusts: community engagement and outreach; environmental friendliness; and responsible entrepreneurship.

Ms Chong believes in a family-oriented culture and in providing staff with a conducive working environment. CSR projects were either initiated by staff through the Staff Recreational Club from the bottom up or driven from the top with management's support. For example, staff who enjoy gardening work take care of the hydroponic farm at the Greenhub building. Everyone in the company is highly encouraged and always motivated to play their part in CSR activities.

Company Culture

The broad strategic objective is to build a High Performance Workforce, focusing on two main goals: to build an innovative culture and develop a talented and multi-skilled workforce, supported by four inter-related human resource processes, i.e. Manpower Planning, Employee and Organisation Development, Talent Management, Reward & Recognition.

An Idiom to Describe Your Business

Seeing Possibilities, Seizing Opportunities.

Instead of working from what is available, Greenpac works from what is possible. From that point of possibility, they can then re-define, re-design and re-engineer a vastly superior solution.

Indoguna (Singapore) Pte Ltd

MD. Helene RAUDASCHL

Company Profile

Indoguna (Singapore) Pte Ltd was established in Singapore in 1993 as a meat company importing the highest-quality chilled meat from all over the world, with affiliated companies in Dubai, Hong Kong and Indonesia. Since then, they have expanded their product offerings to include other premium food products like seafood, fine food and an assortment of artisanal cheeses, chocolates and bakery products. Indoguna Singapore also operates a fully-operational butchery to provide customers with a range of value-added services like meat portioning and processing. In addition, they also carry a flagship brand of premium seafood named Ocean Gems by Indoguna to supply a consistent source of exceptional seafood to countries across Asia and the Middle East. In line with their belief of staying at the forefront of gourmet food trends, they started an online retail arm, Greengrocer.com.sg, in 2007, to meet the growing demand that home consumers have for quality produce. In 2010, they launched a new house brand called Carne Meats by Indoguna which offers specialty meat products like sausages, salami, cold cuts and burger patties in authentic European style.

The company believes in offering a diverse and exciting range of products sourced from all over the world, meeting and maintaining the highest quality standards for food products and offering prices that are competitive in the market place. As a result, clients hail from the professional food community in Singapore, including the island's top hotels and restaurants, gourmet shops, supermarkets and airline caterers. In line with plans to expand beyond Singapore, Indoguna has a state of the art Halal food manufacturing hub in Jebel Ali, United Arab Emirates. Indoguna Productions FZCO produces a range of quality Halal food products, catering to clients in the Middle East and eventually the rest of the world.

Setback

The occurrence of Bovine Spongiform Encephalopathy (BSE), commonly known as mad cow disease in Europe and America — lessons learnt: diversify, diversify and diversify! Never put all of your eggs in one basket.

Must-have Qualities of Successful Entrepreneurs

Believe in yourself, stay focused, and go get what you believe with the most passionate and positive energy.
- Calculated risk takers
- Organised
- Visionaries

- Bend some rules
- Everything is possible
- Be a listener

Turning Point for the Business

Creating a difference with their own house brands:
- Ocean Gems by Indoguna
- Carne Meats by Indoguna

Significant Milestones

1993: Indoguna Singapore Pte Ltd was established

1996: Purchase of first property at 36 Senoko Drive, Singapore

2002: Ocean Gems by Indoguna, house brand of seafood was established

2006: Indoguna Dubai LLC, a joint venture distribution centre in Dubai/ Abu Dhabi was established

2007: Greengrocer.com.sg, an e-commerce website was established

2008: HACCP and ISO9001 certified in Indoguna Singapore.

2009: Carne Meats by Indoguna, house brand of charcuterie and European styled small goods was established

2011: Purchase of 3rd property at 34 Senoko Drive, Singapore.

2012: Indoguna Productions FZCO, a fully owned subsidiary in Dubai, United Arab Emirates, was established

2013: ISO22000 certified in Indoguna Singapore

2015: ISO22301 certified in Indoguna Singapore

2015: Masterpiece by Indoguna, house brand of convenience foods was established

The Next 20 Years

To be an international brand representing passion for products, passion for people, and passion for morality. Abiding by the philosophies of eating well, and consuming preservative free, chemical free, non-MSG products and natural produce. Health is wealth! Price is relevant but not the first priority.

Exercising and eating well are the formulas to wellness! Indoguna believes that providing quality food at good value, bundled with food safety assurances, is instrumental for the business in the future.

Major Contributions to the Economy

- Employment of close to 200 people
- Major contributor as a tax payer
- Contributing to the dynamism of growth in the F&B business in Singapore, and making Singapore one of the best culinary destinations of the world in the recent years

Representing Singapore Internationally

Indoguna Singapore is already exporting to Malaysia, Hong Kong, Macau, Dubai, Abu Dhabi, Mauritius and Egypt under their house brand Ocean Gems by Indoguna. Ocean Gems by Indoguna is a representation of a Singapore brand that is of quality and high food safety standards.

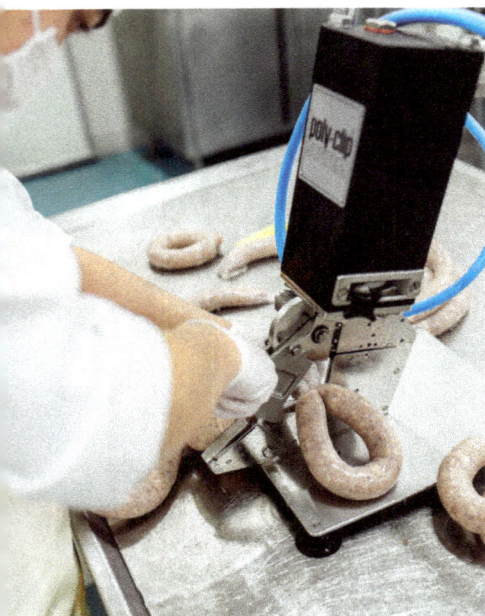

In the near future, Indoguna Productions FZCO will be exporting more products that share the same attributes and values as Indoguna Singapore.

Major Influences and Inspirations

Ms Raudaschl cites her Mother, Elena Tang; Husband, Georg Raudaschl; Son, Maximilian Raudaschl; Sister, Irene Wong and business partner, Elizabeth Liman as her major inspirations.

Name a Local Dish That Best Represents You or Your Business

Chilli Crab, as it represents the attributes of being fiery, passionate, daring, consistent and dependable.

Giving Back

Ms Raudaschl believes that it is important to give back to the industry by nurturing the younger generation to continue the work, and to carry on the legacy well into the future.

Company Culture

The people represents the company's culture and these cannot be taken apart. It is the most basic pillar and foundation to the success of any business.

Jason

Jason Marine
Group Ltd

Chairman Joseph FOO

"Persevere and continue to
pursue your dreams."

Company Profile

Jason Marine Group Limited (Jason Marine or the Group) is a leading marine electronics systems integrator and support services provider for the marine and offshore oil and gas industries. Established in 1976 with its headquarters in Singapore, Jason Marine has since expanded into Indonesia, Malaysia, Thailand as well as key shipbuilding markets such as South Korea and China. It carries an extensive range of products from renowned manufacturers and continues to add products chosen to meet customers' exacting requirements.

The Group's proven expertise in marine communication, navigation and automation systems enables it to offer one-stop solutions that span design, supply, integration, installation, testing, commissioning and maintenance. Jason Marine also provides certification services and sells satellite airtime services to complement its communications business.

Significant Milestones

The first significant milestone was achieved in the 1980s, when Jason Marine moved beyond Singapore and expanded the business regionally into Malaysia, Indonesia and China.

The second significant milestone was attained during the 1990s, when they moved up the value chain and transformed from being a seller and repairer of marine electronics equipment, to a systems integrator providing a full suite of turnkey solutions to customers, including customised and optimised solutions.

The third significant milestone came in 2009 when the Group was successfully listed on the Catalist board of the Singapore Stock Exchange.

Setbacks

The worst setback that Chairman Mr Joseph Foo ever experienced was over-stocking on a particular brand of product which eventually became obsolete. As a result, the company suffered a financial loss.

For him as Chairman and for the Group, it was an important lesson. The company has since learnt to be more prudent and assess market requirements more carefully before committing to any major stock purchases.

Advice to Budding Entrepreneurs

Mr Foo encourages budding entrepreneurs not to give up easily when they encounter challenges during the course of executing their vision and business plan. Persevere and continue to pursue your dreams.

Must-have Qualities of Successful Entrepreneurs

In Mr Foo's opinion, the three must-have qualities are:

* Good values
* Diligence
* Perseverance

Turning Point

The turning point for Jason Marine came when the Group was listed on the Catalist board of the Singapore Stock Exchange in October 2009 — 33 years after the business was founded in 1976.

The listing helped to raise the Group's profile in the industry and propelled Jason Marine to improve its structures and processes, and turn it into a professionally run business today.

The Next 50 Years

In the next 50 years, Jason Marine will be helmed by a competent team of professional managers who will steer the Group to becoming a global player in Marine Electronics.

The industry is moving towards modernisation and digitalisation. It will be more technology-driven and the pace of advancement will accelerate.

Major Contributions to the Economy

- One of the pioneer operators in the marine sector, who has operated and even grown through several downcycles in the sector;
- As an SME in Singapore demonstrating how new HR initiatives* and the adoption of modern technology can propel the company forward; (*won the first SME Employer of the Year award in 2014 by HRMAsia)
- Putting in place, CSR initiatives that will support education and help to improve the lives of the underprivileged in society.

Representing Singapore Internationally

As a successful SME with more than 30 years'of history, Jason Marine has built up enduring relationships with a growing network of suppliers, vendors and partners of different nationalities. They have come to believe and trust in the company. In this respect, they believe they have represented the 'Singapore' brand well.

Name a Local Dish that Best Represents You or Your Business

Chicken Rice. The famous Singapore Chicken Rice is unpretentious. Yet this hot favourite with both locals and foreigners requires the well-blended chilli, fragrantly-cooked pandan rice, and even side condiments like minced ginger and a thick black sauce to bring out the best in the chicken.

Like chicken rice, Jason Marine Group sees itself as an unpretentious organisation, with the full complement of innovative products and dedicated services to appeal to both local and international communities. They have the right people whose winning attitudes have made a difference to the customers.

Giving Back

As a Group, Jason Marine has benefitted from the development of Singapore over the years, and stand ready to give back to society, always remembering the underprivileged who need a helping hand.

The Group has always been actively engaging staff in CSR activities to promote the welfare of the underprivileged over the years. They are encouraged with the positive response and believe that these efforts to build a company with a heart is bearing fruit.

Company Culture

Jason Marine's company culture is centred on three values:

- Character
- Commitment
- Competence

They have provided the compass and have guided the Group's actions and moulded their decisions all these years.

Character is the fundamental quality of a competent and committed company. They believe that if a person has the right attitude, he or she can be nurtured to be a competent team member.

An Idiom to Describe Your Business

Not so much an idiom but a motto that resonates within the organisation — "We are Jason".

Staff are treated like family and are always looking out for each other. They also work as a team work to meet customers' needs to their fullest satisfaction.

We are Jason!

Jason Parquet Specialist (S) Pte Ltd

CEO Jason SIM Chon Ang

"As a young child, Jason had little interest in studying and took 8 years to complete the PSLE."

Company Profile

Established in 1987 as a timber flooring service provider, Jason Parquet (wholly owned by Jason Holdings Limited) is today primarily engaged in the provision of indoor and outdoor flooring solutions with a reputation for and track record of quality and reliability. Jason Parquet carries a range of more than 30 types of timber species to cater to its customers' preferences and budget. Leveraging its extensive knowledge of wood properties and installation methods, the company has supplied and installed millions of square feet of timber flooring for numerous private and public residential and commercial projects. Jason Parquet also supplies and installs environmentally friendly flooring products and "Flor-Deck" wood plastic composite decking.

The company has been awarded Grade L6 by the Building and Construction Authority (BCA) in the Finishing and Building Products category and this allows it to tender for Singapore public sector projects of unlimited contract value. Jason Parquet is also a BCA-Approved Training and Testing Centre, which allows it to carry out training and assessments.

Jason Holdings Limited was listed on Catalist of the Singapore Exchange Securities Trading Limited on 25th September 2012.

Setbacks and Recovery

During the Asian financial crisis in 1997, economies in the region were floundering. Many customers closed down their businesses and defaulted on payment. The company lost nearly S$1 million!

To make matters worse, just as business started picking up, in 2001, the world was hit by the September 11 terrorist attacks. This, coupled with the 2002 SARS episode, were further blows to the business.

Those were dark times for CEO Mr Sim, who regularly found himself working 18 to 20 hours a day to keep the ship afloat. "At that time, I really suffered a lot. Every time I tried to pick myself up, something would come along and cause me to trip again. But I did not give up. My willpower is strong," he said.

Advice to Budding Entrepreneurs

Set short-term and long-term goals for yourself and aim to push yourself to do things that are well beyond your comfort level.

A successful entrepeneur must possess 3Ds — Drive, Direction and Determination. Learn your strengths and apply them, know your weaknesses and mitigate them.

Turning Point

Jason Parquet has come a long way in establishing its position as one of Singapore's leading providers of timber flooring services. The company has grown since its listing on the Singapore Exchange Catalist in 2012. This expansion has served the Group well in terms of increasing revenue as well as enhancing its market position both locally and overseas.

Significant Milestones

Then (1987)
Paid-up capital   : 0
Manpower   : 2
First year turnover   : Negligible

Now
Paid-up capital   : S$5.2 million.
Manpower   : 50 staff, 200 foreign workers and 100 subcontractors
Turnover   : S$36 million (2014)

The Next 50 Years

Jason Parquet have good projects in the pipeline that are expected to contribute positively to the Group's performance. Nevertheless, business is likely to be challenging given the various property cooling measures introduced by the Singapore government. Slow or delays in work progress at existing project sites will result in lost revenue and drive up material and labour costs.

In the midst of this tough environment, the company remains focused on its core projects segment of supplying and installing a comprehensive range of timber flooring under their "Tech-Wood" brand for main contractor and retails customers. They also intend to step up their marketing efforts based on their good track record and reputation. Notwithstanding this, they intend to be more selective by undertaking higher-margin projects and managing subcontracting costs more efficiently.

Jason Parquet will also continue to expand the sales and distribution of timber, WPC, stone products and flooring accessories, both locally and overseas. They have identified China and South East Asia as key potential growth markets and will seek opportunities through strategic investments, acquisitions and joint ventures in these countries.

The current cooling measures and rise in material and labour costs forced some companies to close down or merge. Those who survive will be the strongest and will stay on longer in the markets.

Major Contributions to the Economy

- Collaboration with BCA by setting up BC-Approved Training and Testing Centre for timber flooring.
- Helped construction workforce upgrade their skills and increase productivity in timber flooring sector in line with MOM's objective.
- Created more than 350 job opportunities.
- Market share. Nearly 80% of high-end residential projects which indirectly impacts the GDP of Singapore.

Representing Singapore Internationally

Jason Parquet is a 100% Singapore home-grown brand. They have grown since listing on the SGX and will continue to expand the sale and distribution of timber, WPC, stone products and flooring accessories to overseas markets.

Major Influence

As a young child, Mr Sim had little interest in studying and took eight years to complete the PSLE. He never scored well enough to advance beyond the first year in secondary school and pleaded with his teachers for a second chance but was

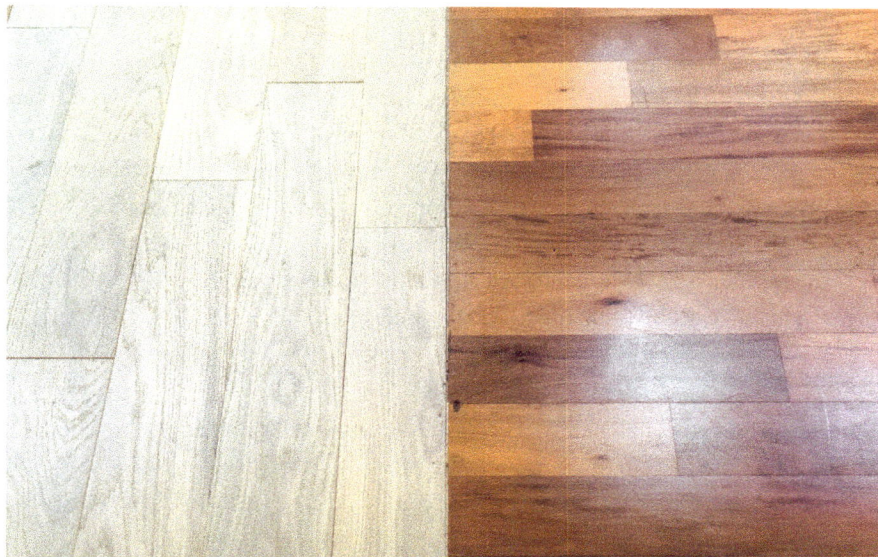

given a flat-out rejection. Instead of holding him back for another year, his teachers advised him to seek out an ITE (then Vocational & Industrial Training Board 'VITB') education instead. Though despondent, he took their advice. ITE matured him to become a very different person. Crucially, his teachers did not give up on him, kept on encouraging him to be the best he could be. "The encouragement has definitely helped me become who I am today". he said.

Giving Back

The company is giving regular support and contribution to charities such as Riding for the Disabled Association of Singapore (RDA), Singapore Children's Society, Association for Persons with Special Needs (APSN), Club-100 @ North-West, schools and temples, among others.

Company Culture

Size up your competition.

In 1986, Mr Sim had foreseen that the veterans of the parquet industry would most likely retire and close their businesses, owing to the lack of succession planning. Today there are less than 30 small players and five giants in the industry. Jason Parquet is one of the market leaders in the supply and installation of a comprehensive range of timber flooring products under the "Tech-Wood" brand. It also sells and distributes timber products and flooring accessories.

Treat Your Employee Right

Mr Sim leads a faithful and dedicated team. He ensures that the company runs on an efficient operational system complying with ISO requirements. This, in turn, ensures that there is no major overhaul of work processes after annual quality audits, minimising workflow disruption. His employees are therefore always taken care of, knowing that they are part of a company that will not compromise.

He also believes in maintaining a responsibility-based corporate culture, where teamwork thrives. Through teams, his employees are able to work together effectively while at the same time, develop multiple skills.

Know Your Product Well

Mr Sim and his Sales Team always carry all the wood samples with them whenever they meet potential clients. With the real samples, clients can see, touch and feel the different types of wood and sense the aroma. This means the Sales Team can better explain each type's unique qualities.

An Idiom to Describe Your Business

Walk Your Talk!

JEP Precision
Engineering Pte Ltd

CEO Joe LAU

*"It is imperative for entrepreneurs to
continue learning and upgrading their skills."*

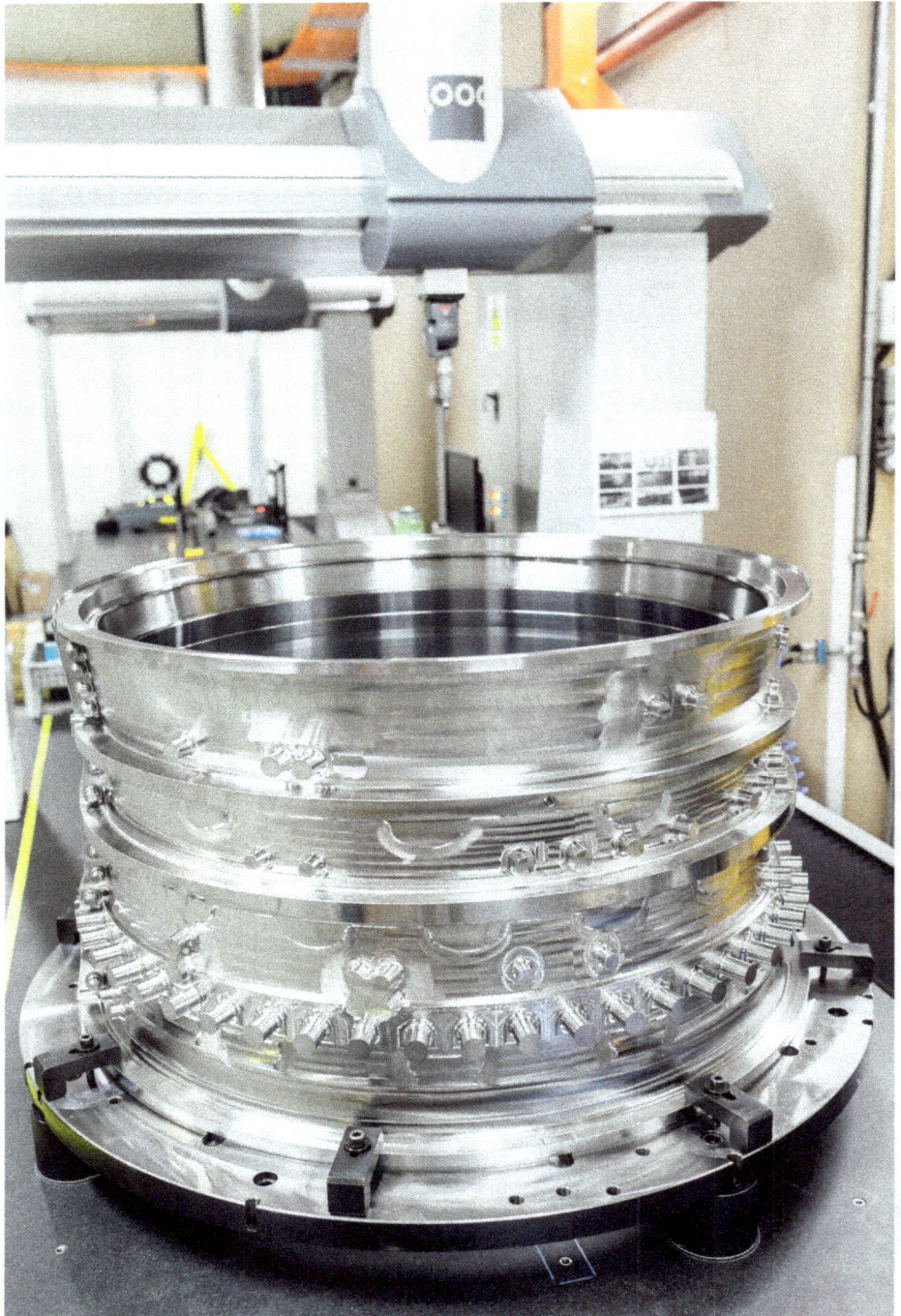

Company Profile

Established in 1990, JEP offers high quality-machined products for the Aerospace, Oil and Gas and Machine Tool Industries. From humble beginnings, they have grown over the years from a small workshop into a manufacturing facility that covers a land area of 120,000 sq ft.

Today, JEP are a leading sub-contractor for the local aerospace industry. They also provide a highly integrated service to customers; offering full turn-key projects from material sourcing, fixture designing, machining of components as well as special process.

Milestones

Over the years, JEP have developed a strong team who are experts in their field, loyal and willing to work hard towards the company's vision and goals.

Through sheer hard work and dedication, JEP were able to move up from a second tier supplier to a first tier one, supplying parts directly to Aerospace OEMs like Messier-Bugatti-Dowty, United Technologies Aerospace Systems, EATON and MOOG.

The next milestone will be doubling its size in the next three years, to stay competitive while keeping operations based in Singapore.

Setbacks

To date, there have not been any major setbacks for the business. However, a downturn in business was experienced during the global economic crisis in the early 90s, 1997 Asian financial crisis and currently, in a market of falling oil prices.

Through such experiences, JEP say they have learnt to be always prepared for business cycles through constant work, productivity and financial planning.

Advice to Budding Entrepreneurs

It is imperative for entrepreneurs to continue learning and upgrading their skills.

Besides being equipped with knowledge on the relevant business market, it is equally important to work on other areas such as Finance, Marketing and Customer Relationship.

Starting a business is the easy part. The challenge is to manage the growth and continuation of the business.

Must-Have Qualities of Successful Entrepreneurs

Passion, Optimism, Resourcefulness and Hard Work.

Turning Point

The turning point for JEP came in 2005 when the company became profitable and two new shareholders invested in the business, namely EDBVI and Singapore Aerospace Manufacturing (SAM).

In 2006 the company generated a turnover of S$17 million and a profit of $3.6 million.

To date, the company has grown from an operation of 100 staff to 240 staff and from a production space of 10,000 sq ft. to 120,000 sq ft.

The Next 50 Years

JEP hopes to progress into design, development and manufacturing of technology-intensive complex components.

Additive Manufacturing may be the game changer in the next 50 years.

Major Contributions to the Economy

- Moved Singapore up the value chain by attracting more complex and high value-added manufacturing in Aerospace and Oil and Gas components.
- Supported the supply chain in manufacturing of precision engineering components.
- Increased workforce in Precision Engineering sectors.

Representing Singapore Internationally

With a strong passion for this business, the goal is to position JEP as a sought after world-class supplier for high quality precision-machined products for the Aerospace and Oil and Gas industries.

Name a Local Dish that Best Represents You or Your Business

Chicken rice, one of Singapore's global iconic dishes.

Giving Back

Yes. Other than donations, JEP participates actively in the training institutes to train and promote Precision Engineering as a career path to support one of the key pillars in our economy: the manufacturing sector.

Company Culture

JEP believes in a team-centred approach. They value cohesion, open communication and a participative working environment. This teamwork is important to the success of the company as it helps to keep the morale high and staff connected with their work.

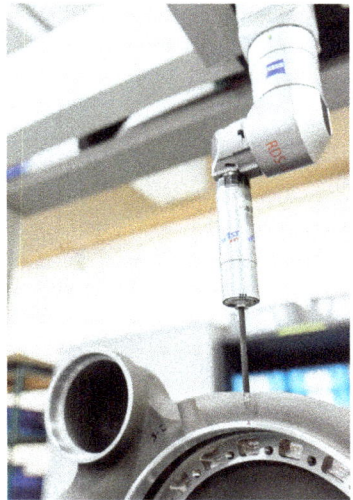

An Idiom to Describe Your Business

The sky is the limit.

JP Nelson Equipment Pte Ltd

Chairman: Nelson LIM

"The company believes that people are their first and most often quoted accomplishment."

Company Profile

Established in 1992, the Company leases, sells and services equipment for engineering, construction, oil and gas, and offshore industries. Since its beginnings as JPN Equipment with 60 staff members, it has transformed into a regional powerhouse with over 400 employees and operations in Australia, Hong Kong, Malaysia, Taiwan and Thailand. As our Chairman Mr Nelson Lim puts it: "We believe that instead of waiting for opportunities, we should create them. Holding firmly to that tenet since the Company's conception, we are always exploring opportunities, and unwavering in our pursuit of excellence and innovation. We have an emphasis on fairness and meritocracy. Upgrades and training programmes constantly better the competitive edge of our employees, and we believe that the Company grows with its people. From our Chairman to our professional engineers, the loyalty and pride of our staff manifest in many ways, such as the humble but meaningful tradition of donning our Company shirts on a daily basis."

Business Lessons

危机, 先有危后有机。Every obstacle and challenge faced is an opportunity in disguise. JP Nelson was a small player in the equipment industries back in the 90s. To differentiate themselves from fellow competitors, JP Nelson chose to focus on one of their core strengths, which was to deliver the best customer service possible. To be different, JP Nelson set out to not just lease equipment, but also offer solutions like machine repairs and the provision of spare parts. JP Nelson never ceases in its mission to enhance its capabilities and services. Hence the management team are always sourcing for new and improved machineries for the construction industry. The aim is to continue enhancing, provide modification as well as refurbishment of existing machineries to support the change in environmental needs and demands.

Advice to Budding Entrepreneurs

Persevere. As Steve Jobs had said, "I'm convinced that about half of what separates the successful entrepreneurs from the non-successful ones is pure perseverance."

Must-have Qualities of Successful Entrepreneurs

- An unwavering passion
- Open-mindedness
- A forward-looking approach

Significant Milestones

- Listing on the Taiwan Stock-Exchange
- Expanding across the ASEAN region including Malaysia, Hong Kong, Taiwan,Thailand as well as Australia

The Next 50 Years

Efficient and space-conscious construction methods will come to the fore in the decades ahead and our machines must evolve with it. The emphasis on green technology will also be a challenge for existing construction machinery providers.

Community Outreach

JP Nelson is a member as well as sponsor of a yearly event organised by the Metta Welface Association (Metta). The association is founded by Venerable Shi Fa Zhao, Abbot of the Golden Pagoda Buddhist Temple. The company has been providing service-in-kind such as generators as well as donations towards the association since 2000.

Metta is currently providing welfare services to the less fortunate that includes: Disability Care, Medical Care, Children Care as well as special education for children with mild intellectual disability.

The staff from JP Nelson are highly encouraged to participate. Prior to the event, the company goes the extra mile by providing EDMs, posters as well as "food coupons" for staff to bring their family to attend the annual celebration.

In 2015, JP Nelson started to collaborate with Young NTUC to play a part in some of their events. One project is RUN350 where the main focus is in reducing carbon discharge and to grow the green movement. This has particular relevance to JP Nelson as they are in the construction industry, where heavy machineries emit high level of pollutants into the environment.

The event held by Young NTUC, RUN350 has a vision similar to JP Nelson — which is to reduce pollution. In April 2015, JP Nelson became the official equipment sponsor for the events.

"The company's culture is about ordinary people creating extraordinary results."

Company Profile

Since Koufu's establishment in 2002, they have held on to the Chinese belief that it is one's good fortune to feast on good food. The company's mission is to provide good food and a level of service that customers are able to enjoy while sticking to their deep roots in traditional Singaporean cooking in the true coffee shop tradition.

Koufu's logo represents the company's commitment to make a difference in the world through its food. Koufu's mission statement, "Better Food, Better People, Better Life", describes how it strives to bring about a warm family ambience whilst serving the best food to customers, thus creating an unsurpassed and fulfilling lifestyle experience.

Milestones

In 2003, when Koufu acquired several good foodcourt locations, this led to huge progress in the business between 2004 to 2006.

In 2010, they opened Rasapura Masters at Marina Bay Sands (MBS). This was a milestone given that Koufu started out in Singapore's heartlands. It is a proud achievement to venture onto the international stage with a food court located at the renown MBS.

In 2012, the first overseas Koufu food court opened in Macau, bringing the uniquely Singaporean concept of a modern food court infused with the local coffee shop tradition overseas.

Setbacks

The selling of Yuhua in 2000 was the most memorable setback. The lessons learnt were that it is important to constantly innovate as well as to adapt and move along with the times. This also means keeping a lookout for new business opportunities.

Advice to Budding Entrepeneurs

Concentrate on building your core business and be hardworking. Build and lead an outstanding team, constantly innovate, have a vision and be clear of the company's positioning.

Turning Point

In 2003, when the economy was affected by SARS, Koufu acquired quite a few good sites for its food court business. It turned out that those sites were acquired at a good price due to the economic downturn during the SARS period.

The Next 50 Years

So long as Singapore continues to sustain its economic growth, Koufu is confident that the foodcourt business will also flourish.

But challenges abound. There will be more choices in the market which will allow people to have more healthy options with the growing awareness of healthy eating.

Major Contributions to the Economy

- The creation of jobs for more than 1000 employees.
- The changing of people's traditional perspective of the F&B industry. In the past, F&B was associated with being a low-paying industry. However, as stated in Koufu's mission statement — Better Life, Koufu believes in offering good employment terms to enable staff to have a better life.
- Koufu has also been providing opportunities for businesses in other industries, by growing their supplier and vendor base. Many vendors have grown with them over the years and a strong relationship has been established.

Representing Singapore Globally

Koufu endeavours to bring the Singaporean coffee shop tradition to the rest of the world, by raising awareness of the uniquely Singaporean custom in which food, fun and family go hand in hand. The multi-cultural and multi-national elements of Singapore's society are also brought to the fore in this respect.

Name a Local Dish that Best Represents You or Your Business

The bun set, which comes with kaya-butter bread, two eggs and one cup of Nanyang coffee best represents the business.

MD Pang Lim, a Hainanese, is familiar with the traditional Nanyang coffee, which was brought to Singapore by the early Hainanese immigrants who themselves picked up the coffee roasting technique from the Westerners whom they worked for. Made from fine coffee beans that have been roasted with sugar and margarine, the caramelised and buttery aroma of the brewed coffee retains a smooth texture when sipped.

The traditional bun set is a very popular item which is sold at all Koufu outlets. Many customers love the bun set and have it for breakfast or tea. Koufu sell more than 10,000 sets of traditional buns every day. The Nanyang-inspired traditional coffee is well-loved by customers for its smooth texture and aroma, which goes perfectly well with the eggs and freshly-toasted bread that comes with butter and kaya.

Giving Back

Koufu believes a country's development is connected to its people. It is imperative to close the gap between the rich and the poor in order to have a successful business. A society with good well-being is required too. As part of Koufu's efforts to be a socially responsible company, they support initiatives benefitting the less fortunate and elderly, and have participated in numerous relevant activities and events.

Company Culture

The company's culture is about ordinary people creating extraordinary results. Having developed from a small and traditional company to one of the largest food court operators in Singapore, Koufu's success is proof that so long as one is willing to learn, he can create extraordinary results.

An Idiom to Describe Your Business

In Chinese it is called, 与时俱进, meaning to constantly adapt, improve and move along with the times.

Money World Asia Pte Ltd

MD Agnes SIAW

*"One should never give up
and never feel embarrassed
to seek help!"*

Company Profile

Money World, a 24 year-old company, is one of the most trusted and reliable remittance houses in Singapore. They serve their clients based on the 3S motto – Security, Speed, and Service.

They are supported by a pool of clients mainly from multinational corporations, listed companies, small and medium enterprises and high net-worth investors. They have expertise in handling the global forex market and currencies such as the G7, Chinese Renminbi, Indonesian Rupiah and the Malaysian Ringgit.

Significant Milestones

In 1991, Money World started out as a numismatic company dealing with collectibles and commemorative products. That's where they built the relationships with major banks around the world as well as the Board of Commissioners of Currency-Singapore (BCCS).
In 1997, they coordinated the Commemorative Notes to mark the handover of Hong Kong to the People's Republic of China. Again in the same year, 1997, Money World was licensed to start the remittance business.

Setbacks

The main setback was getting the right candidates to reform the company when the regulatory demand was taking place a decade ago. It encouraged Ms Siaw to concentrate on making a decisive breakthrough along the way.

Advice to Budding Entrepreneurs

One should never give up and never feel embarrassed to seek help! With the right attitude, passion and perseverance, you hold the key to your success story!

Must-have Qualities of Successful Entrepreneurs.

To excel, we have to be adaptable, passionate and persistent.

Turning Point

The turning point for the business came with the active participation at the Handover of Hong Kong to the People's Republic of China in 1997, where Money World coordinated the commemorative notes to mark this momentous occasion. Since then the company has focused on the world of money remittance.

The Next 50 Years

Ms Siaw foresees that the business will grow beyond just a remittance house. Currently, they are working towards a one-stop financial service centre for clients, extending their current FX products and services to share financing, mini-bonds, equity crowdfunding, e-wallet, and an online or mobile payment system.

The remittance industry will gradually evolve; these days, investors have become more sophisticated and tech savvy. Perhaps in the next 50 years, people will go cashless, and trade payments would be made using legalised virtual currencies, like Bitcoin.

Describe three Major Contributions to the Economy

Firstly, remittance boosts the economy by facilitating the FDI and inter-companies transactions for multinational corporations.

Secondly, it also eases the collection of income and payment to overseas counter parties for local businesses.

Lastly, it encourages foreign investors to move their wealth here for the purpose of investments and businesses.

Representing Singapore Internationally

At Money World, they have a robust compliance system, a good regulatory environment (regulated by the MAS), and a good payment framework (partnering with major banks in Singapore). These criteria give confidence to investors and entrepreneurs to conduct business safely in Singapore.

Major Influence and Inspiration

The late Michael Jackson — Ms Siaw says she was inspired by his perfectionism and never-give-up attitude.

Name a Local Dish that Best Represents You or Your Business.

Hainanese chicken rice — a simple dish which is catered to everyone's appetite but no one does it better than us. It is prepared using our own in-house secret recipe!

Company Culture

The company has a team of energetic and vibrant employees. They focus on work efficiency and also value work-life balance! And yes, these are important qualities for a successful business!

An Idiom to Describe Your Business

"Be on the ball". In this business, it is very important to be up to date on the current industry regime and be attentive towards clients.

Nordic Flow Control Pte Ltd

CEO: Dorcas TEO

"My grandfather's entrepreneurial spirit inspired me as I witnessed how he painstakingly built his fortune from scratch"

Company Profile

Nordic was established in 1998 as an automation system integration solutions provider serving mainly the offshore and marine, and oil and gas industries. Through continued organic growth and mergers and acquisitions, we have grown into a group providing services such as System Integration, Maintenance, Repair and Overhaul (MRO) and Trading, Precision Engineering, Scaffolding Services, as well as Insulation Services. Nordic Flow Control Pte Ltd, a subsidiary of Nordic Group Limited (a listed company on the Singapore Exchange), which is headquartered in Singapore, has facilities in China and representatives worldwide. We turn systems into solutions by providing innovative automation solutions for vessels and platforms by designing and developing multifunctional systems as well as offering servicing, engineering assistance, and installation to over 100 customers worldwide.

Significant Milestones

In 2004, Nordic established its presence in China, which expanded our business overseas, and mitigated country – concentration risk.

In 2011, Nordic acquired Multiheight Group and expanded into the scaffolding business, which mitigated the risk associated with concentration in only the offshore and marine sector.

In 2015, Nordic acquired Austin Energy and expanded into the insulation business. The acquisition gives an immediate order book and earnings accretive, and offers a gateway for Nordic to provide services to the fast-growing pharmaceutical sector. The synergy between the insulation and the scaffolding businesses is expected to stimulate the order flow.

Setbacks

Ms Dorcas Teo says a personal setback changed her life forever. When her father passed away in 1996, she witnessed first-hand how her mother, a housewife, had to work and take care of the family on her own from then on. Her siblings and herself were still schooling at that point and it was not an easy task to bring them up all by herself.

This really changed Ms Teo's perspective on life and she learnt that as a woman, she needed to be independent.

Advice to Budding Entrepreneurs

Develop a never-give-up attitude; if you fail, just climb back up and walk again.

Must-have Qualities of Successful Entrepreneurs

* Integrity
* Passion for your business
* Courage

Turning Point

The Group has been growing on a steady basis over the last 17 years. Ms Teo hesitates to label any major milestone on the company's growth as a "turning point"; rather, they were built on assets and expertise, a diversified revenue stream.

The Next 50 Years

Nordic has achieved notable growth through major diversification processes in the past few years. We had a target to reach annual revenue of S$100 million, and with the recent acquisition of Austin Energy, we expect the target to be achieved soon.

Nordic will continue to monitor the market, study potential mergers and acquisitions opportunities, and acquire successful businesses when appropriate, with a focus on the business that is relevant to us and within our footprint, that offers the potential to broaden our product and service range in Marine, Oil and Gas, Petrochemical and Pharmaceutical sectors, and that offers the potential to create synergy with our existing businesses and stimulate future revenue and profit growth. With both organic growth and expansion through mergers and acquisitions, we will strive to grow Nordic into a strong company with diversified revenue streams, a stable customer base, appropriate geographical presence, steady revenue and earnings growth. Also, a listed company has the capability to reward shareholders on a consistent basis.

Despite the weak market for the oil and gas, and the offshore and marine industry following the sharp and prolonged decline in oil prices, studies show that the demand for oil and gas will continue to grow in the long term, given the population growth and energy demand globally. At the same time, oil and gas reserves will remain limited. The business cycles for these industries will eventually have an upside, and the system integration, MRO and trading scaffolding and insulation businesses will embrace better times.

Customers will also prefer an integrated service provider with a broader product/service range, and the recent acquisition of Austin Energy is one step towards catering to this trend.

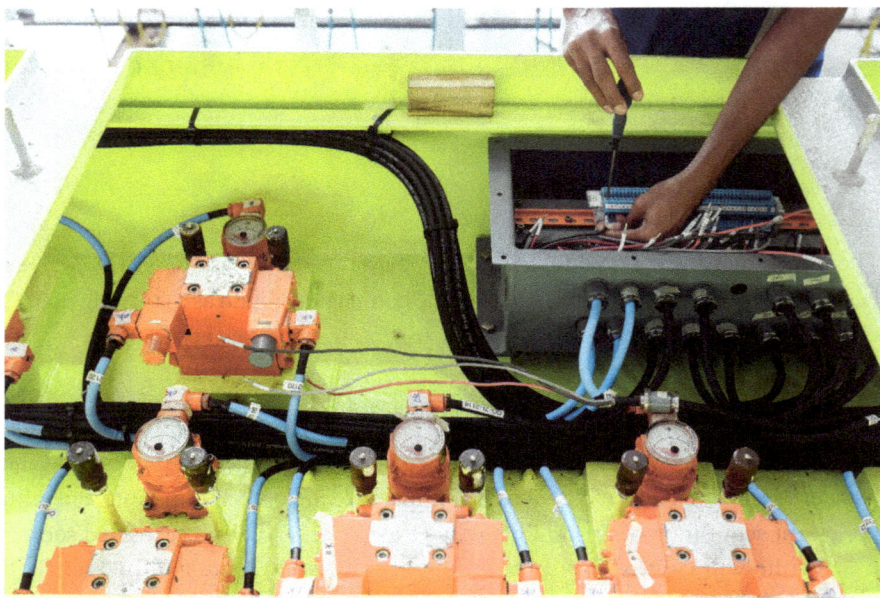

Major Contributions to the Economy

Nordic has filled in the demand for the various products and services in the offshore and marine, and oil and gas industries on the market, provided jobs for more than 1200 employees, and rewarded shareholders with an increased dividend payout.

Representing Singapore Internationally

Nordic's integrated systems are used for many vessels, such as oil tankers, oil rigs, container ships, and drill ships, all over the world. This affirms our position as a Singaporean brand on international platforms.

Ms Teo believes the Group's scaffolding and insulation services can represent Singapore given the sheer number of safety awards they have won, which indicates quality, trustworthiness and high standards. As for precision engineering, the in-house design and engineering capabilities highlights the advanced skill sets of Singapore's educated workforce.

Major Influence and Inspiration

A major influence for Ms Teo would be her grandfather, who came all the way from China in search of a better life in Singapore. She remembers when she was very young, he would wake up at four in the morning to cycle from Payar Lebar to Punggol to buy fresh eggs. The total travelling time was four hours! He sold those eggs at his provision shop, which was set up at the front of the house. He also allocated a large portion of the house to be rented out. His entrepreneurial spirit inspired her as she saw how he painstakingly built his fortune from scratch.

Name a Local Dish that Best Represents You or Your Business

Bak Chor Mee because this uniquely Singaporean dish is a balanced combination of different flavours that harmonise wonderfully, just like the different components of Nordic Group.

Giving Back

It is essential for companies to contribute to the community in any way they can offer and we would like to encourage this. It is not only about giving back to the community; it also encourages bonding among employees.

For Christmas last year, instead of having a typical celebratory lunch or dinner, the two subsidiary companies under Nordic Group, Nordic Flow Control Pte Ltd and Multiheight Group went down to AWWA Community Home for Senior Citizens to celebrate with the elderly.

Company Culture

The following values make up the culture of the company. Ms Teo believes these values are essential to the success of the business as people are the core strength of Nordic.

- Nurture
- Ownership
- Respect
- Discipline
- Integrity
- Collaboration

An Idiom to Describe Your Business

Keep our fingers on the pulse.

At Nordic, we believe that we should always be attentive to our environment, and do this by staying vigilant of the market developments. We always have an ear to the ground to ensure we stay ahead of the competition.

This allows us to make superior advancements and constantly raise the bar in quality, technological creativity and productivity.

OKH Global Ltd

CEO Thomas BON

"Developing New Business Opportunities and Interlinking Strategic Investments in Asia and Beyond."

Company Profile

Established in 1998 and headquartered in Singapore, SGX-mainboard listed OKH Global Ltd. ("OKH" or "the Group") is an integrated property developer with a strategic focus on logistics and industrial properties.

With a market-oriented business model, the Group is interlinking its strategic investments with its capabilities in property development to further strengthen its business presence in Asia and beyond.

Memorable Setbacks and Lessons Learnt

When I took over OKH, the Group had severe cash flow problems as the Asian Financial Crisis had resulted in a slowdown of business and bad debts resulting from clients. Rather than wasting precious time and effort to collect the residual bad debts, I decided to change tack and source new clients even though I had little means to finance new projects.

However, I convinced these new clients to prepay (as much as possible) for work and also brought them to meet suppliers so they could pay the suppliers directly. Both initiatives helped to solve the cash flow issues and at the same time, built a good working relationship with suppliers (who later provided better credit terms for my future projects).

This episode highlighted the importance of resourcefulness in a company. In order to build such traits within OKH, a collective team effort is required. In line with the expansion of OKH's business activities, human capital is an important foundation to facilitate and build sustained growth. Hence, my strategic priority is to attract suitable, like-minded individuals into the organisation to enhance the business model, extend competitive strengths and market presence.

Advice to Budding Entrepreneurs

- Create a meritocracy-based structure: OKH is like a close-knitted family organisation, although none are related by blood. I believe in meritocracy and staff (new and experienced) know that performance and contributions are highly regarded, hence they seek to continuously enhance their knowledge and capabilities to better value-add to customers and business associates.

- Build cohesive teamwork: Part of our strong growth is through the cohesive teamwork within the Group. With a hands-on approach, the management team come together quickly to resolve the pertinent business and operation issues on hand.

12 Tai Seng Link, artist impression

- Implement process-driven framework: As OKH expanded progressively, I recognised that our focus and response time slowed down correspondingly; hence I implemented a system and process management approach in business activities so co-workers are empowered to make quick and sound decisions within a designated system/process established. This helps to quickly identify potential issues and resolve them in a timely manner.

Must-have Qualities of Successful Entrepreneurs

Courage: To believe in oneself and pursue the ideas/dreams
Perseverance: To continuously put in hard work and forge ahead when the challenges seem unabated
Adaptability: To change/refine the business model when the operating environment evolves

Turning Point

My business vision for OKH has always been in Property Development.

The turning point for the business was our first property development project, Seatown Industrial Centre, in 2009, which coincided with the global credit crunch. It was a daunting period as the Group's accumulated financial resources were

ACE@Buroh, artist impression

substantially tied up in this project.

Instead of feeling despair, I rallied the team to go down to the sales office to educate the property agents on the merits and rationale behind the development. This initiative proved to be very successful as the agents were empowered with the knowledge and they were able to share them with potential buyers, leading to the successful sell-out of our first property development project.

Since then, OKH continue to deploy this same strategy and that has led us to capture a commanding presence in Singapore's industrial property market.

Significant Milestones

In 2013: Successful listing on SGX mainboard

In 2014: Joint venture with Pan Asia Logistics to develop, own and manage modern logistic properties across Asia

In 2015: Acquired a 15% stake in established logistics and supply chain firm, Pan Asia Logistics, to serve European MNCs in Asia

The Next 50 Years

In the next 50 years, I believe that property development will still be a core part of the business.

However, OKH will endeavour to broaden our presence in other property segments such as logistics, warehousing and commercial spaces. Once we have a foothold in these market segments, we will seek to deepen our reach and strengthen our competitive advantage.

To further diversify and extend the business model, OKH may also undertake acquisitions, joint ventures and alliances to tap new business synergies and business opportunities.

Property development is as old as human civilisation as everyone desires a roof over our heads. However, from time to time, we have seen how new technologies and ideologies evoke new market trends, leading to a paradigm shift in consumer preferences.

Having said that, I foresee that over the next 50 years, there will be more property development projects in Singapore and Asia with eco-friendly features to save energy and create energy at the same time. In addition, building designs will be more complex to suit the expanding lifestyles of an urban population.

Major Contributions to the Economy

Business enterprises, big or small, are important to the Singapore economy as we have limited resources. More importantly, SMEs in Singapore can bring growth and innovation to the community in which they are established. For OKH, we recognise that the design of industrial properties in Singapore is simple, outdated and boring, hence we set out to change this perspective with aesthetic facades, eco-friendly features and contemporary interiors for our industrial property development projects. Even though it would cost more to design and construct, tenants in these specially-designed industrial projects could enjoy a conducive working environment while serving the various functional requirements of their businesses.

From then on, other new projects began to follow the new market trend. Notably, some of OKH's projects have been accorded design and eco-friendly awards that are on par with other well-known residential and commercial properties.

I am humbled by the fact that the perception of industrial

Woodlands Horizon

properties has improved and business owners who utilise such industrial spaces can have a well-designed and functional working environment to be more productive and enhance their corporate branding.

As a business enterprise, OKH contributes to economic growth by providing fair employment opportunities to people from all walks of life. Lastly, through corporate culture and initiatives, we hope to foster entrepreneurship within our organisation and business partners to improve productivity and growth.

Representing Singapore Internationally

I believe OKH has the capability to respond and adapt quickly to changing market trends in a global landscape.

When it comes to design innovation, it really depends on our resourcefulness and not so much on the resources at disposal. For example, despite being conceptualised and developed locally in Singapore, our property development project, A'Posh BizHub, has won various design and building awards in the international arena.

As a Singapore home-grown company, we have the unique advantage of strong corporate governance, transparency and bilingualism. This is particularly important when Asia is emerging as the driver of the global economy and these unique advantages have undoubtedly widened the Company's capabilities and laid the foundation to expand our business presence in the international arena.

Evident from the logistics and supply chain business ventures, we have already connected established MNCs to emerging markets in Asia. Given the small domestic market, overseas markets will be a natural way for OKH to create new opportunities for stake-holders and add long-term sustainable value for shareholders.

With the rise of emerging markets in Asia, I believe that the company can leverage on solid business foundations in Singapore and establish ourselves as a globally competitive company.

A'Posh BizHub

Major Influence and Inspiration

Singapore's founding father, the late Mr Lee Kuan Yew, is a major influence and inspiration to me. Despite limited resources, his foresight and perseverance to develop Singapore into a world-class country and economy has raised Asia's standing in the global arena, bringing together the best qualities of the East and West economies.

Likewise, as a home-grown Singapore company, I aspire to develop OKH to be a globally recognised and respected firm.

Loyang Enterprise, artist impression

Name a Local Dish that Best Represents You or Your Business

Our business is akin to a famous local dish, Bak Kut Teh. It is an intensely flavourful and delicious dish enjoyed by both the locals and overseas visitors. Looking deceivingly simple, this rich, savoury and fragrant food requires a systematic and sophisticated mixing of herbs, spices and pork ribs to ensure consistency in quality.

Hence, this dish best represents our business belief that we must ensure consistency in our ability to value-add to our stakeholders and to uphold the strong corporate values expected of a Singapore establishment.

Giving Back

For OKH, every company, large or small, is part of a community. And we believe that being a good corporate citizen will deepen our roots in the community and we in turn benefit indirectly in the following ways:

- It creates a "feel-good" feeling for employees as giving back to the community reminds us of how lucky we are.
- Through community involvement, we have developed quality relationships that have helped in other ways not foreseen.
- People want to work for companies that care, hence it has enhanced the HR recruitment programme as the Company expands.

Hence, while proactively managing OKH's business activities and expansion plans, I am also committed to have the Group undertake a growing role in giving back to society by supporting various corporate social responsibility and environmental conservation programmes in the community. On a personal level, I have donated S$2 million to Ren Ci Hospital to support their health-care initiatives to the poor and needy.

Company Culture

The Company's culture is centred on OKH's vision statement "To build iconic, sustainable and eco-friendly buildings with excellence in construction and safety standards".

This vision statement is a pivotal tool in success and growth as it keeps our management team and staff focused and motivated towards a common objective.

On the Company front, this vision has been incubated and entrenched as part of our corporate culture and work principles. We have to recognise fellow colleagues' efforts, implement appropriate incentive systems and most importantly, upgrade their technical skills via training to empower them with the capabilities relevant for this purpose. Over time, these initiatives translate to increased empowerment with a strong sense of corporate identity among the workforce.

Through an open sharing working attitude, OKH adopts a market-oriented approach towards our business. Aligned with new market trends, we continuously seek to innovate, improve service and quality while keeping costs low.

Prime BizHub

An Idiom to Describe Your Business

I abide by the Chinese saying: "宝剑锋从磨砺出，梅花香自苦寒来", which means, hard work and determination are the basic ingredients of success.

Oilfield Supplies & Services Pte Ltd

Deputy MD: Kay ONG

"An entrepreneur has to be an all-rounder in all aspects of operating a profitable company."

Profile

Oilfield Services and Supplies Pte Ltd ("OSS") manufactures and services high quality down-hole tools and drill stem components that are used primarily by the oil, gas and mining exploration and production industries.

Since the company headquarters' inception in Singapore in 1999, OSS has met the dynamic needs of the drilling industry and complied with tighter tolerances required for many innovative and complex products. Today, OSS distributes a wide variety of down-hole drilling products all over the Asia Pacific and the Middle East Regions. OSS has been supporting Singapore's vision to be Asia's Premier Oil hub for the past 15 years by offering critical turnkey manufacturing support and auxiliary services to service companies and drilling contractors which have established their regional headquarters and central sourcing functions in Singapore, with a strong presence internationally as well.

A Humble Beginning

The company's major influence and inspiration is the Singapore Government which has always stressed to all that "no one owes us a living". One has to be resilient. OSS founder and CEO Mr Peter Ong had minimal support during the company's start-up, with the knowledge that the staff's livelihood was directly dependent on his every action and decision. The journey was a tough one, progressing from being a wage earner for 20 years, to an entrepreneur with monthly overheads to worry about. The early days with an initial team of just three staff in a rented 3000 square feet workshop next to a rubbish collection company remains a great memory. They would secure any work available and pick their brains to ensure that it was done to the full satisfaction of their customers. That is the spirit which has kept the company afloat for the first three years.

Qualities of Successful Entrepreneurs

In the early days, Mr Ong worked for various MNCs which gave him the insights and a platform to start his own business. This experience has taught him that an entrepreneur has to be an all-rounder in managing all aspects of a profitable company to ensure it is financially sound at all times. He has to be responsive to emerging trends in the market and be able to see into the future as a multitude of opportunities rather than unforeseen obstacles.

One also needs to lead by example, to be directly involved in the company's daily operations and inspire the entire team to take ownership of their respective

jobs and stay committed to the success of the company.

Most importantly, he ought to share the fruits of the labour with all employees where it is due.

Key Qualities

- Lead by example to have all staff collectively work towards the company's common goals.
- Be prudent and financially strong to tide over difficult times and be ready to embark on any great opportunities on the horizon swiftly.
- Gain the trust of customers in ensuring that their goals are met with satisfaction. It is of paramount importance that products' quality and services stay relevant to stay ahead of the competition.

Turning Point

The huge turning point for OSS was the awarding of certification by API (American Petroleum Institute), a non-profit organisation which acts as a governing body for companies directly involved in manufacturing and servicing for the Industry. This paved the way for new opportunities that were previously unachievable due to the tight restrictions set in place by the global Oil and Gas Industry.

Other significant turning points that were instrumental would be the awarding of a factory space by JTC back in 2006, at the Kian Teck site, which is over 21,000 square feet. This is in stark contrast to the old days when OSS was in just a rented factory shared between two companies in Loyang. Besides the improvement in aesthetics for a positive first impression on customers, the increased space also allowed OSS to expand our workforce along with additional machines, concurrent with our venture into the manufacturing sector at that point of time.

Significant Milestones

- Awarding of the (API) American Petroleum Institute licenses to manufacture and service Oil and Gas products for drilling service customers.
- Qualification by customers to be on their approved vendor lists.
- Building company's infrastructure that is in line with the growing demands of the market, along with the necessary equipment and qualified personnel needed.

Major Contributions to the Economy

Oil and Gas / Shipbuilding and repairs was considered a sunset industry some years ago in Singapore. Ironically, it turned out to be one of the major and most consistent contributors to Singapore's GDP. Oil rig builders like Keppel and SembCorp have effectively placed Singapore on the world map, attracting foreign investors into Singapore, bringing along with it a multitude of business opportunities.

The Oil and Gas industry has created a significant amount of jobs for the economy, with professionals taking home a higher than average salary in comparison with other industries. OSS, being a pioneer and key auxiliary supplier of directional drilling tool parts in Singapore, along with activities for oil exploration in this part of the region, has influenced MNCs to shift their manufacturing line from the US and Europe to Singapore, owing to logistical and cost advantages coupled with high quality assurance. OSS has managed steady growth in revenue of 10% to 12% for the past five years with a decent 15% to 18% PAT.

Representing Singapore Internationallly

Satellite Workshops

During their 17 years in business, OSS has in place a total of eight API approved workshops in the regions namely, three in Thailand (Songkhla & Sattahip), two in India (Mumbai & Kakinada), one in China (Tianjin), 1 in Indonesia (Jakarta) and one in Malaysia (Labuan). They all represent OSS Singapore on an international platform, and are all held in high regard by customers.

OSS grew leaps and bounds after obtaining their API licenses and customers' approval. Luck, good decisions, staff support and perfect timing all play an important part in their success.

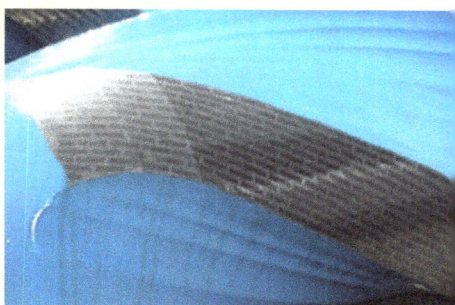

In short, their achievements mirror Singapore's success as they were in a similar situation as Singapore in the 50's. The founders did not have extra money (paid up capital was only S$150K) with a monthly overhead of S$20K that would have lasted them not more than six months. Failure was staring them in the face if they did not have the determination to succeed.

Name a Local Dish that Best Represents Your Business

"Hokkien Mee" is a local dish that is affordable, with a smooth gravy to mix with the ingredients and is filling for hungry stomachs. Ingredients are relatively cheap, easily available and nothing goes to waste as even the prawn shells are blended to make the tasty stock for the dish.

OSS's business model is identical to this dish, as one does not need to go to a culinary school to know the basics before you can whip up a good "Hokkien Mee". The procedures are straight forward in nature with the ingredients all pre-cooked to be mixed with the noodles. This business can be started with low capital investment as equipment need not be new, and no fancy decorations are required to woo customers. All we had were some die-hard friends with trust in OSS that they (the customers) will not have food poisoning after eating our product. Business will blossom through word of mouth when the quality of food and services are up to standard.

Both OSS and "Hokkien Mee" do not require a degree in rocket science to be successful. The essence is to give customers the best quality, reasonable pricing, impeccable service and have the ears and drive for improvement to stay ahead of competitors. The most important element in success is sheer hard work and the determination to succeed.

Company Culture

Meritocracy has been a hallmark of the company since its inception, with a good mix of different ethnic groups comprising of Singaporeans and foreigners, working harmoniously together. These employees proudly hold supervisory positions. One example is Acting Production Manager, Hassan Abdul Moyed Jamir Uddin. He started as a casual labourer and through hard work and determination, managed to upgrade himself and get his ITE level 3 in metal machining and is now pursuing his diploma. The company has always backed and encouraged staff who want to upgrade themselves.

The company was set up with the guiding principles of a family-oriented company whereby there would be no discrimination on race and between Singaporeans and foreigners, in terms of benefits and promotion prospects. Progress is purely based on meritocracy. Turnover of staff in Singapore and the

foreign group of companies are well below the countries' industrial standard, and OSS attributes this success to staying true to our guiding principles and mission.

OSS is now in gliding mode with the occasional turbulence. Charity should start at home (staff) as they are the ones who have their hands on the steering wheel of the company. OSS is currently embarking on an educational bursary fund for well-deserving staff members.

The Next 50 Years

Aligned with the company's vision and goals, OSS aims to continue to grow and remain dedicated to customers. To be prepared for any dynamic changes within the volatile Oil and Gas industry, OSS will have to venture into different markets, and become a globally recognised name for manufacturing and service solutions.

The Oil and Gas industry will continue to provide energy for a very long time to come, with alternative energy still a far cry from reality. The present infrastructure of under-developed countries is still in dire need of vast energy resources which can be tapped on from established companies that have ample resources. It is much more cost effective and can turn out to be a big revenue generator for resource-rich countries to take advantage of this for their economy.

"Pursue Our Dreams with Sheer Determination to Succeed"

Pollisum Engineering Pte Ltd

CEO: ANG Ka San

"Pollisum Engineering focuses on delivering quality service over speed."

Company Profile

Pollisum Engineering was initiated in 1984 with just a sole employee. Today, it has nearly 200 employees at its disposition. The company has evolved from providing simple repairs and servicing to become a One-Stop Integrated Service Provider with a core focus in:

- Leasing and Sales of Heavy Lift and Haulage Equipment
- Fabrication of Construction Buckets, Steel Structures and Engineering Works
- Repair and Maintenance of Cranes and Crane Booms
- Sales and Trading of High Tensile Steel Pipes
- Providing Waterfront Services

The company is renowned for its highest standards of services, and has been awarded the Enterprise 50 in 2013 and 2014 consecutively and the Singapore SME 1000 award. It has also attained various certifications, including the ISO 9001:2008, SS 506 Part 1:2009, BS OHSAS 18001:2007 and BizSafe Star certification — all testaments to its commitment to quality, efficiency and safety.

Setbacks and Recovery

Despite Mr Ang's prominence in the industry, setbacks are still inevitable. When they first started, Pollisum faced many difficulties handling customers of a large scale. The problem worsened as they operated 24 hours daily. They also met with some financial difficulties at the start. But Mr Ang's extensive network meant he was able to join forces with some friends from the same trade and hire more workers.

Pollisum Engineering focuses on delivering quality service over speed. At times, by trying to speed up work, it might hinder their progress in the process. They also maintain a policy of not rejecting customers in the belief that nothing is too big for them. They believe in building rapport with all clients, providing good service and hence build up a relationship with them in the process.

Such proficiency has allowed Pollisum Engineering to do what is deemed unthinkable to most, such as fixing a crane which was already beyond repair. With dreams of attaining greater heights, Pollisum Engineering started hiring salesmen in 2010, after 26 years of operations.

Advice to Budding Entrepreneurs

You must have passion, desire and belief.

Passion is a big thing. If you're ambivalent or mildly enthused about your product or service, that's not going to sustain you through the highs and lows that will inevitably occur. If you find something you love enough to want to share it with

others, that love will fuel and give you purpose.

We all have dreams but if you have a desire to achieve those dreams then this can really push you on in life. The main thing is to believe.

If you believe in yourself, your own ability to make a difference, you won't go wrong. Too many people try to "put you down" in life but if you believe in yourself, it will give you the confidence you need to succeed in life.

Must-have Qualities of Successful Entrepreneurs

- Resilience — Entrepreneurship is going to dole out constant challenges, some of which you've already considered but many of which you'll never see coming. And it's about more than just business opportunities and obstacles – your personal life will be challenged as well. You'll face complex financial problems, decision-based dilemmas, long hours, sudden changes, and predictions that egregiously fail. Triumphant entrepreneurs battle their way through difficult obstacles.
- Forward-looking — Successful entrepreneurs are always thinking ahead. They may stray from their roadmap, and that's okay, but they have one in mind. Having a clearly established set of goals will keep you from getting stuck. Your goals may be constantly evolving, but if you don't know where you want to go, chances are, you won't get anywhere. You need to be a man of your word.
- Take action — Remember business means business and if you keep sitting on the fence you will always be the watcher. To be a successful entrepreneur you

must choose which side of the fence you want to jump over to and make the most of it. Do not ponder on all the pros and cons of a problem too much and delay important projects. You must be a quick thinker and act fast. When necessary make a choice, take action and deal with all the obstacles as they come. Be productive. Sitting around and waiting for things to happen is not going to make you a successful entrepreneur.

Turning Point

Since its humble beginning, Pollisum has sought to differentiate itself by offering a service that is both reliable and responsive, complemented by impeccable customer service. This emphasis on reliability and responsiveness has been the reason for Pollisum's current success, making it a force to be reckoned with in the arena of crane and heavy equipment supply as well as fabrication and engineering services, both in Singapore and the region.

With perseverance, they have managed to not only tide over difficult times, but made their first major breakthrough in 2007. Pollisum were heavily involved in the Resorts World project and out of the 40 units of cranes that they owned, 22 units were deployed and 17 units were working daily.

That was only the beginning of a growth spurt. Major projects such as Marina Bay Sands, Gardens by the Bay, Exxon Mobil Refinery Plant started to roll in one after the other.

The company is still making waves with its continuous expansion into the marine, offshore and construction industries, bringing with it the same reliability and responsiveness that has propelled its remarkable growth thus far.

The Next 50 Years

Pollisum intends to expand into overseas markets and will embark on a marketing strategy of increasing sales by offering a larger scope of operations, tap on and undertake a wider work scope for existing and new customers, thereby creating value and growth for both local and overseas businesses.

Major Contributions to the Economy

Pollisum contributes in terms of scale and share in the development process of necessary public infrastructure and private physical structures for many productive activities such as services, commerce, utilities and other industries.

The company is not only important for the finished product, but also employs a large number of people (directly and indirectly) and therefore has an effect on the economy.

Representing Singapore Internationally

Pollisum intends to expand into overseas markets and intends to embark on a marketing strategy to increase sales. This will be achieved by expanding operations and tapping on a wider scope of customers.

The construction industry is in an expansionary mood in anticipation of a slew of infrastructure projects in Singapore and these projects could demand greater capacity from crane rental companies like Pollisum. As such, they have gradually increased their fleet of vehicles in anticipation of demand to keep in line with their business model as a highly cost-efficient supplier.

Pollisum plans to diversify from land to marine, providing customers with a wider range of services. They are able to utilise their waterfront facilities to offer sea transportation, fabrication, modification, overhaul servicing and repair works, and carry out general loading and unloading of bulky machinery and cargo, with arrangement of land transportation, and/or temporary storage.

Major Influence and Inspiration

Li Ka Shing.

Name a Local Dish That Best Represents You or Your Business

Coffee, because it has evolved from a traditional simple cup of coffee in a kopitiam to a high-class concoction made and appreciated by connoisseurs alike in upmarket cafes.

Giving Back

Pollisum firmly believes that while their businesses are driven by earnings, one must also have a positive impact on society, the community, employees and all other stakeholders. In this regard, the company has constantly strived to contribute to communities where they operate, from touching lives, protecting the environment, championing safety to leading best practices in corporate governance.

They engage and nurture communities wherever they are, with the aim of achieving a sustainable future together. This, they believe, encourages employees to be responsible citizens who are concerned for the well-being of others, especially the less fortunate in society. As such, employee volunteerism is a key thrust of the company's community engagement programme.

Company Culture

The ability to tide through the global economic crisis fully intact is a testament to the success of the operations and internal structure of Pollisum. To further enhance its operations, the company will continue to improve expertise, resources and capabilities while establishing a strong workforce and skills development standards through total training and upgrading programmes. Continuous Quality Improvement Programmes shall be inplemented, while various IT enabled administrative and production processes shall be incorporated as highlighted above to bring the new business model into an unprecedented level of competence.

Pollisum believes that every single staff forms one part of the solid root that runs deep beneath this organisation. Young, bold and with over 30 years of combined experience in both the local and international construction market, each and every individual is committed to the Pollisum vision and mission.

An Idiom to Describe Your Business

The art of good management lies in the capacity to accept change, and the ability to meld new and traditional thinking.

Rotating Offshore Solutions Pte Ltd

The Management Team

*"Cash is king. Contracts can be won but
cannot be delivered without cash."*

Company Profile

Rotating Offshore Solutions design, fabricate and commission oil and gas solutions for clients ranging from asset owners to oil and gas minors and majors. Their three business divisions include package, fabrication and EPCIC.

- The Package division provides package solutions like gas engines, gas compressors and pump packages.
- The Fabrication division fabricates structures weighting up to 3,000 tonnes.
- The EPCIC division engineers, procures, constructs, installs and commissions assets like Mobile Offshore Production Units (MOPU).

These complementary divisions provide one-stop solutions to clients.

Setbacks and Learning Lessons

Cash is king. Contracts can be won but cannot be delivered without cash.

Rotating Offshore Solutions had won and delivered the biggest contract in the entire operating history of the company in 2013. However, cash flow was negative for the project and they managed to deliver the work successfully only with the support of all stakeholders including clients, suppliers, bankers, employees and government agencies.

Advice to Budding Entrepeneurs

We only live once. Give yourself a chance to prove that you can do it. If you try and fail, at least you tried. If you try and succeed, it would not have happened if you had not tried in the first place!

Must-have Qualities of Successful Entrepreneurs

- Think outside the box. If you remain in the same industry, you are just a commodity. Differentiate and the chances of success will be higher.
- Experts are there to help you. We cannot be a master of all trades. Be honest with yourself. Focus on what you are good at and hire experts to focus on what you are not good at. Many entrepreneurs are afraid of hiring experienced staff who are smarter than them. This is wrong.

Hiring experts will enable the business to scale up faster and provide better quality solutions to clients.

- Never give up. There are bound to be lots of problems in business. Solve them or else it will grow and destroy the business. Sometimes, it is overwhelming. Never give up. Just break it down into smaller problems and seek help whenever needed. All problems must be solved. They will not be solved by themselves.

Turning Point

The big break came in 2013 when the company secured their first EPCIC project for a Mobile Offshore Production Unit and delivered it in record time. The market recognised this remarkable achievement and allowed them to grow their track record.

Significant Milestones

- Securing the waterfront yard deal from JTC in 2012. This was important for Rotating Offshore Solutions to grow as with it, they subsequently set up their Fabrication division and EPCIC division.
- Securing the first EPCIC project for a MOPU under the EPC division.
- Securing the first Module project under the Fabrication division in 2015.

The Next 50 Years

Rotating Offshore Solutions hope to grow their Singapore base into a research and engineering hub with similar construction and integration hubs in different parts of the world.

The oil and gas sector has taken a beating since the third quarter of last year. To survive, the company has had to move up the value chain by embarking on more complex projects to maintain their competitive edge.

Major Contributions to the Economy

Rotating Offshore Solutions secure and execute projects out of Singapore. As their solutions are mainly exported worldwide, they believe they in turn add value to the domestic economy.

The business carries with it the Singapore brand as their global clients know that the main business operations are based in Singapore.

Major Influence and Inspiration

General Electric. By focusing on cutting-edge technologies and mergers and acquisition, GE has grown into a global powerhouse. Learning from this, the company hopes to use similar strategies and grow.

Giving Back

The company has been supporters of HSBC's All In A Day's Work for years. They believe it to be a great way of helping the less fortunate and involving staff in meaningful causes at the same time.

Company Culture

Never give up. It is important to find out-of-the-box solutions for clients. This is never easy but one should never give up.

An Idiom to Describe Your Business

The ball is firmly in your court.

One has to add value and help their clients. Their problems are our problems. We have to find solutions to their problems in order to ensure our continued survival.

"The most important assets of a company
are its track record and people.
With a strong track record, Ryobi Kiso is
well positioned to excel and grow
its business across various markets."

Company Profile

With a track record of 25 years in ground engineering, Ryobi Kiso Holdings Ltd. ("Ryobi Kiso" or "the Group") is a leading solutions provider, specialising in eco-friendly piling and geoservices including environmental protection engineering and geotechnical engineering products and services. On 27 January 2010, Ryobi Kiso was listed on the Mainboard of the Singapore Exchange Securities Trading Limited ("SGX-ST"). Ryobi Kiso is one of the few ground engineering contractors in Singapore registered with L6 financial grading with the Building and Construction Authority (BCA) of Singapore, allowing it to tender for public sector piling projects of unlimited contractual value.

As a leader in innovative ground engineering solutions in Singapore, the Group has completed more than 500 projects in the public and private sectors comprising residential, commercial, institutional, industrial, infrastructure and environmental protection projects. In the 1990s, Ryobi Kiso was among the pioneers in Singapore to introduce eco-friendly piling technologies and equipment such as Screwed Spun Piling and Press Grouted Spun Piling. In 2007, it was also one of the few companies in Asia outside Japan to commercially deploy the patented Trench cutting and Remixing slurry Diaphragm wall ("TRD") machine for Environmental Protection Engineering projects. In January 2012, the Group expanded its core business to include property development, trading and investment.

Business Lessons

In recent years, like many players in the local construction industry, Ryobi Kiso made a conscientious decision to seek outward regional expansion beyond the Singapore market. In the midst of this regional expansion, the Group has experienced some challenging scenarios. For instance, there were cultural differences for each region, which required in-depth understanding and strong adaptability by the company's staff to ensure the smooth operation of the projects. Also, rules and regulations pertaining to the industry are very different in each market and these require time and effort to acclimatise to each situation and customers' needs.

Due to the capital and technologically intensive nature of the business, Ryobi Kiso has to become flexible and versatile in the deployment of resources in their regional pursuit. The Group optimises its resources to capture various opportunities in the different countries, while also paying close attention to the needs of the local customers.

Advice to Budding Entrepreneurs

All budding entrepreneurs should have the following attributes:

- Perseverance
- Diligence
- Calculated risk-taking

"There are always ups and downs in a business cycle, so it is important that you learn to manage your expectations during a down-cycle," remarked Mr Ong Tiong Siew, Chief Executive Officer and Executive Director of Ryobi Kiso ("Mr T.S. Ong"). The above-mentioned traits have allowed him to overcome many challenges and enabled his organisation to emerge stronger and larger after each trough of a business cycle.

He lives by this saying: "Remember, when your business hits a high, be humble and always remember your roots. But when things are not going smoothly, bite it and persevere as there will always be a breakthrough. Stay determined, have courage and work hard."

Turning Point

In the business of ground engineering which is a highly regulated industry, Ryobi Kiso needs to attain high standards of checks and pre-qualification before each project is awarded.

Through many years of hard work and delivering quality projects, Ryobi Kiso's major turning point arrived when it finally achieved a L6 grading from the Building and Construction Authority of Singapore, allowing the Group to tender for public piling construction projects of unlimited value in Singapore. At that point in time, Ryobi Kiso was one of the few companies which was awarded such grading.

Over the years, Ryobi Kiso has built up a solid track record of high-profile projects such as Sentosa's link bridge, Sentosa Gateway Tunnel, MRT Downtown Lines 1 and 2, SIA Airbus 380 aircraft hangar and SASCO aircraft hangar in Changi Airport, Yong Loo Lin School of Medicine, Duke-NUS Graduate Medical School, Institute of Technical Education @ Simei, Marina Costal Expressway, Punggol Waterway, NUS University Town, Esperance Port Access Corridor in Western Australia, and many HDB projects.

These projects require a high level of engineering expertise due to their complexity. Their public projects track record has also led them to succeed in the private sector, securing many prominent projects such as LASALLE-SIA College of the Arts, Goodwood Residences, the Trillium, Singapore Island Country Club, Park Regis Singapore, The St Regis Singapore, Mediapolis@One-North, Medical Technology Hub, SSG Towers One and Two at Ho Chi Minh, The ONE at Ben Thanh Ho Chi Minh, Saigon Golf and Country Residences at Ho Chi Minh, King Squares 1, 2 and 4 in Perth, Perth Busport, Capital Square in Perth, and many others.

Significant Milestones

There have been many major milestones in Ryobi Kiso's journey, and the most significant, in Mr T. S. Ong's opinion, are the following:

- The collaboration with Japanese partners during the founding years, and the technology transfer to Ryobi Kiso;
- The introduction of environmental-friendly piling technologies in the 1990s and 2000s; and
- The initial public offering of the Group in January 2010.

The Group got off to a good start as they identified a need for advanced piling technologies and engineering expertise. In 1990, following a partnership with Mr Shuntaro Shiga, the founder of Ryobi Kiso Co Ltd, they established Ryobi Kiso. The company thus became the only local company then to possess large diameter rock boring capabilities in Singapore. Additionally, it paved the way for a successful fusion of over 50 years of Japanese pioneering excellence as well as their own knowledge of Western piling technology.

Another key milestone of the Group was in the early 90s when they started to introduce new eco-friendly piling to the Singapore market. The first environmental friendly project was the Gold Coast Condominium project at West Coast Road where they introduced the large diameter non-reinforced Grout-Mix Piling technique to construct the temporary eart-retaining structure. They believe they were among the pioneers to utilise such an eco-friendly technique in Singapore. Today, they are one of the fore-runners of innovative eco-friendly piling solutions.

The Group's initial public offering in 2010 further strengthened financial stability and enhanced their brand name. Achieving a listed status has aided expansion into overseas markets as it lends stronger credibility to the Group, especially when they tendered for major and high profile projects. Since then, their presence has expanded beyond the Singapore market and has reached Australia, Malaysia and Vietnam.

The Next 50 Years

Ryobi Kiso believes in the enormous potential for growth even in the next 10 to 20 or even 50 years.

They believe the main success factors are their core values of technological innovation, adaptability and the relentless pursuit of value-add for customers. These core values are the pillars of the Group's success and they believe they will continue to serve them well into the future.

The Group has continued to innovate and evolve, adding more services to its business. In addition to its main activities of bored piling, eco-friendly piling and geo-services, the Group has diversified into property development and systems engineering and process automation.

The Group has expanded its property core business and made investment both in Singapore and overseas.

Going forward, Ryobi Kiso will continue to grow their core and new businesses while monitoring the market and technological trends so as to calibrate their business models to remain relevant, sustainable and competitive. As the ASEAN countries continue to collaborate regionally, more markets will continue to consolidate and the competition will get more intense. While more competitors will enter their traditional Singapore market, the Group can also move into other regional markets, expanding their geographical presence. As such, Ryobi Kiso envisions more Singapore companies will become more regionalised and even globalised as they are poised to leverage on the good Singapore branding in project management, safety emphasis, technological leadership and professionalism.

Notably, they believe ASEAN will be undergoing a rapid expansion of infrastructure projects as the governments promote connectivity to facilitate trades and commerce.

Within the Singapore market, they envisage that the increasing population and the higher population density will continue to generate increasing demand for high-rise buildings and underground facilities. This will mean a need for more engineering advancement in piling and ground engineering.

Productivity and automation will be another critical area of focus. More companies and businesses will be exploring technologies or equipment that can help to lessen their reliance on human resources as the nation continues to focus on improving efficiency and productivity.

Major Contributions to the Economy

Mr T.S. Ong recaps fondly that the company has been fortunate and honoured to participate in the building and transformation of Singapore. Being a player in the construction and infrastructure sector, they have contributed to the rapid urbanisation and the improving skyline of our beloved nation.

During the 1990s, Ryobi Kiso was among the pioneers to introduce new ground engineering solutions to the local market, which has helped to improve productivity and efficiency in our sector. With the successful transfer of technology know-how industry wide, the local industry players have benefited and the overall industry has progressed.

Moreover, they have also brought in eco-friendly piling solutions, which involve earth-friendly and low pollution piling works with minimal noise, vibration and soil removal, as well as savings in raw materials. These environmentally friendly solutions have resulted in economic cost savings such as the reduced need for additional pollution control, and for rectifying structural damages to nearby buildings or properties.

Another major contribution to the economy is the Group's direct involvement in key mega infrastructure projects such as Marina Coastal Expressway, Punggol Waterway as well as the Group's recent participation in the Thomson East-Coast MRT Line.

Representing Singapore Internationally

Singapore has always been an efficient country with strong regard for safety, innovation and adaptability. These are also the traits and values of the Group. In Ryobi Kiso, there is strong belief in innovation and emphasis on productivity and efficiency.

Above all, the Group does not compromise on safety. Strong emphasis is placed on maintaining a safe work environment. At the same time, its staff is expected to deliver good results, quality work and to provide value-added solutions for stakeholders.

Being a Singapore company brings growth opportunities and recognition in overseas markets. Ryobi Kiso hopes to showcase their innovative and customer-orientated culture to overseas customers, thereby further reinforcing the good image of a Singapore company.

Major Influence and Inspiration

Mr T.S. Ong cites his grandfather as a major influence and inspiration. The elder Ong did not have the opportunity to receive an education as a child even though he came from a small town in Fujian province of China that had produced a prime minister in the Qing Dynasty.

The elder Ong worked as an apprentice in a bean curd shop instead, and joined his mother in Singapore when he was sixteen years old. They started a small business dealing with bean sprouts. He worked hard and the business expanded and eventually he became a major supplier to the British Army families, merchants and residents residing in the Tanglin Road area, supplying daily produce and groceries.

As a teenager, Mr T.S. Ong had the opportunity to hear his grandfather's views on business and his opinions on current affairs. He also brought the young Mr T.S. Ong along on his rounds to meet his friends and business partners. He was a trusted and upright person who earned respect and support from the business community. Mr T.S. Ong admires and draws inspiration from his grandfather's success in building up a business from scratch through hard work, trust, acumen and perseverance during difficult times.

He also admires the great philanthropist, Mr Tan Kah Kee for creating job opportunities for the community, helping the poor and contributing to society, especially in terms of education for the poor. The elder Ong had also donated generously to the building of schools and amenities in the villages, both in Singapore as well as in his birthplace in Fujian, China. Mr T.S. Ong also admires his ability to self-study. He had always placed great emphasis on education. He believed that education would be the best gift for his children, especially for his daughters when women were not given a fair chance to get an education.

He is also an excellent model of self-learning and life-long learning. Even though he was not educated formally, he was able to read classical Chinese literature and communicate effectively in writing with friends and family members. This was rare in those times for the underprivileged.

Name a Local Dish That Best Represents You or Your Business

Dim Sum — value for money, wide variety and always prepared with passion.

Company Culture

The Group believes in helping customers find practical, well-researched and cost-effective solutions. Every member in the company is committed to provide reliable and innovative solutions and add value to customers.

While Ryobi Kiso strives to deliver excellence and quality to customers, developing employees to achieve personal growth and success is also key to sustaining the business. Training, self-development and lifelong learning are ongoing facets of organisational development.

This culture of personnel development has served the Group well as the most important assets of a company are its track record and people. With a strong track record and talented staff, Ryobi Kiso is well positioned to excel and grow its business across various markets.

An Idiom to Describe Your Business

There is a Chinese saying: "万丈高楼平地起". Similarly, Ryobi Kiso believes that whatever they do, a strong foundation is most important, and this has been the cornerstone of their success.

"Dare to dream, even if the dream
seems impossible to everyone else."

Background

Established in 1988 and listed on the Mainboard of the Singapore Exchange since July 2000, Serial System has developed a distribution network built on strong partnerships with its suppliers and customers. In 2014, Serial System crossed the US$1 billion revenue mark, making it the largest electronic components distributor in Singapore.

Serial System has a diverse range of customers from industries such as consumer electronics, household appliances, industrial manufacturing, telecommunications, electronic manufacturing services, automotive and medical. Its major suppliers include Texas Instruments, Avago Technologies, ON Semiconductor, TE Connectivity, Advanced Micro Devices and OSRAM Opto Semiconductors.

The company is well established in Asia, where it has more than 1000 employees, 58 offices and 10 warehouses. Its markets comprise Singapore, Bangladesh, Cambodia, China, Hong Kong, India, Indonesia, Japan, Kazakhstan, Malaysia, Philippines, South Korea, Taiwan, Thailand, United Arab Emirates, Vietnam and Australia.

In addition to distributing components, Serial System also endeavours to boost demand for these products by adding value to them through design and other initiatives. This has made the company an integral part of the supply chain, where it is able to bridge the gap between suppliers and manufacturers, shortening their time to market.

Today, Serial System is entering a new phase of growth as it ventures beyond its core competencies to distribute finished consumer products. Its current portfolio of finished goods includes lifestyle and consumer electronics products like timepieces and printer accessories, as well as household appliances. The company is also expanding its geographical network to head into new markets such as Australia, the United Arab Emirates, Kazakhstan, Bangladesh and Cambodia.

Setbacks

Serial System may have come a long way since its inception, but its journey has not been easy. In 1999, Dr Goh relinquished his CEO position, a move that unwittingly took a heavy toll on the company in the following two years. The company lost close to S$50 million after its new CEO decided to venture into the manufacturing and distribution of finished consumer electronics, a business that required huge capital outlays.

Determined to nurse Serial System back to health, Dr Goh stepped back into the CEO role. He took several years to recover the losses the company suffered but

also learned a valuable lesson — finding a successor requires careful planning and should never be rushed.

Turning Point

After recovering from the fallout, Dr Goh decided that the company needed to expand beyond Singapore in order to reach greater heights. In the following years Serial System pursued a number of joint ventures and acquisitions in South Korea and Greater China. These initiatives enabled it to ramp up its businesses and develop better economies of scale. Today, Serial System has an extensive distribution networks in first-, second- and third-tier cities in China, among other markets. This accomplishment enabled it to generate the milestone revenue of more than US$1 billion in 2014.

Corporate Culture

Dr Goh has made it a point to empower his employees to perform to the best of their ability by providing them with the right resources and work environment. This has served the company well, and makes it easier for him to oversee the company's vast operations in 18 countries.

The Next 50 Years

Despite being one of the leading distributors of consumer electronic components in Asia, Serial System sees itself growing even bigger in the next 50 years. According to Dr Goh, demand for electronic devices and equipment can only grow. "As such, electronic components for these devices will continue to be sought after. Scale is definitely a key factor for success in this business and Serial System needs to be bigger to achieve greater economies of scale."

As it scales up, the company may also go big on e-commerce. "Global procurement and shipments are becoming more transparent worldwide. On-line purchasing will be the norm. Serial System may even manufacture electronic devices and venture into other businesses to drive growth in future," says Dr Goh, who would like to see the company generate US$30 billion in revenue over the next five decades.

Contributions to the Economy

Besides Serial System's achievements, Dr Goh also takes pride in the Group's contributions to the economy. These include the more than 1000 jobs it has created in Singapore and abroad. He also takes pride in the fact that Serial System, a

homegrown company, is able to work with leading global semiconductor brands such as Texas Instruments, Avago, ON Semiconductor and Osram.

Major Influence and Inspiration

Dr Goh cites his mother, who worked very hard to support the family as an influential figure in his life. Having experienced poverty at a young age, he learned to be strong and independent, and worked hard even as a child to earn some money to help support the family. It was his mother who taught him to give back to society when he finds success — a teaching he has closely followed over the past 20 years and imbued in Serial System.

Giving Back

In just the last year alone, Serial System donated S$676,000 (US$523,000) to various organizations in Singapore, including the five Community Development Councils (CDCs) and the Singapore Children's Society. It also contributed S$50,000 to charitable foundations and schools, such as the National Kidney Foundation, Ren Ci Hospital, the Breast Cancer Foundation and Nanyang Polytechnic, to support medical awareness programmes.

For the past two decades, Serial System has celebrated every Lunar New Year at Tai Pei Old Folks Home, distributing goodie bags as well as red packets, bringing festive cheer to the elderly with traditional lion dance performances.

In conjunction with its 25th anniversary, Serial System and Zhi Zhen Tan Dao Xue Hui, a Taoist charity organisation founded by Dr Goh, pledged in November 2013 to donate S$150,000 each to the five CDCs over three years. On their part, the CDCs will match the donations dollar for dollar between 2014 and 2016. The total donations of S$4.5 million over that period will be used to encourage active living among the elderly, promote lifelong learning, and groom youths to become future leaders of Singapore.

A Local Dish that Best Describes You or Your Business

Mixed vegetables rice! "The wider the range of dishes, the better for consumers. Just as different diners would have different preferences, different electronic devices

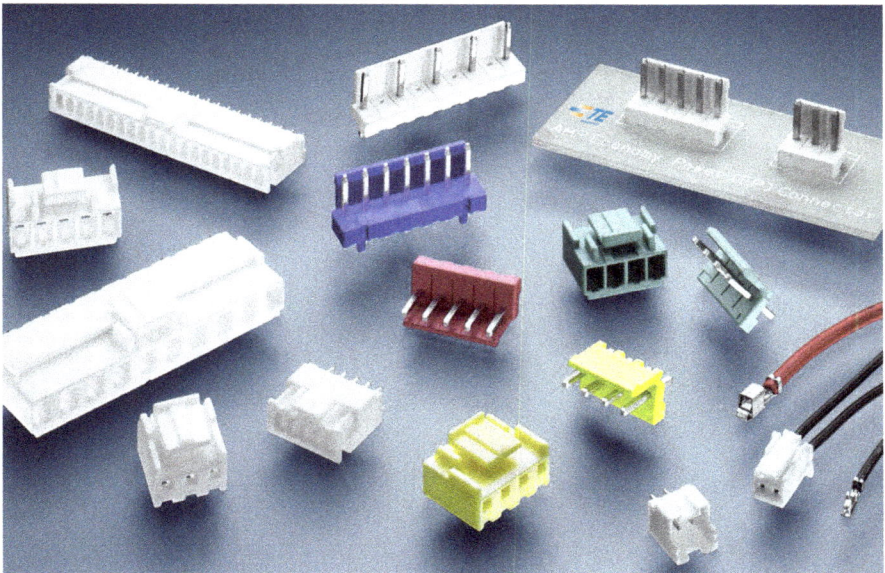

would require different types of components," says Dr Goh.

"To run a mixed vegetables rice business, one would need a large variety of dishes, ranging from meat to fish to vegetables, to offer a complete meal. Prices would be higher for meat dishes and lower for vegetables. This is similar to the components distribution business, where different parts are needed to complete an end-product like a TV set or a mobile phone, and the parts would cost more for certain chips and less for common components."

Advice for Budding Entrepreneurs

To anyone aspiring to be an entrepreneur, Dr Goh says the individual must first dare to dream, even if the dream seems impossible to everyone else. "Entrepreneurs see opportunities everywhere. They are innovators who are always on the lookout for opportunities." Clear objectives must then be established. While it is important to be disciplined and stick to what has been decided, perseverance is key, especially when the going gets tough, he says.

"When things don't go as planned, you have to persevere and be determined to start over again if necessary. You should be prepared to take risks, live with uncertainty, and be able to adapt to change." Beyond that, an entrepreneur should read and travel widely and network extensively, he adds. Once the business is established, it is important to plan for succession to ensure continuity, he says. For that, the company has to invest in talent development.

Silver Bullion
Pte Ltd

CEO Gregor GREGERSEN

"Entrepreneurship is about creating value for customers. Do something that people will appreciate enough to pay for."

Company Profile

Silver Bullion buys, sells, tests and stores physical precious metals in Singapore. The team have a Banking and IT background and over the last six years have developed many processes, insurances and protections that make them the safest place to store your silver and gold.

Their definition of "safest" includes legal, jurisdictional and counterparty protections that large global storage providers cannot provide. These factors have made them successful with a small number of well-educated individuals.

Setbacks

Personally for CEO Mr Gregor Gregersen, the largest setback occurred during the dotcom bubble, when he spent 15 months to successfully develop and license a timeshare booking system to a third party company in California, only to see the company fail and go bust in 2001.

On the bright side, the project taught him valuable technical and project management skills. It also taught him to look at the bigger picture and the importance of timing. A company can be worth hundreds of times more if it strategically fulfils a need at the right time.

So it pays to understand the big picture, re-verify assumptions and make practical strategic decisions based on this. Most people do not know how to look at the big picture because it requires a lot of work and will typically follow popular trends instead.

Advise for Budding Entrepreneurs

- Create value - Entrepreneurship is about creating value for customers. Do something that people will appreciate enough to pay for and is not already done better by somebody else in your area. Never do what everybody else is doing because there will be too much competition and you will add only little value.
- Test your business idea and have a plan B.
- The beginning is often the hardest so it is best not to throw too many resources into your business idea until you know it will work. Opening a store in a place like Singapore for example is a major financial commitment that could easily end in disaster. So first retail a product through cheap alternative means such as a website. If the website does not work you will still have resources to try something else.
- Look for alternative uses before you make a major commitment. For example, find ways to allow for subletting a store before signing a lease so that you can

exit your commitments if needed. Also, if you spend years of your life on a project make sure you can sell your "experience" on your resume.

- Do what you have a passion for.
- If you have a genuine passion for your business you will probably be good at it and willing to invest the long works hours required. If you are not committed then don't bother starting a business.

Must-have Qualities of Successful Entrepreneurs

- Persistence, a business is more like a marathon than a sprint.
- Honesty, you must persistently create genuine value for somebody. No cheating or tricks as it will destroy your reputation.
- Focus on your niche, be very good at something specific so that you have a competitive advantage in your small sector. You are too small to be a generalist.

The Future

Silver Bullion did not have a huge turning point. The company has been profitable from the start and never had to take any external debt. Instead, since inception, they have continuously worked on improving on their weaknesses and consolidating their strengths which resulted in carefully planned and gradual improvements.

Mr Gregersen believed that, if they look for a turning point, it lies in their

future because they have structured the company and products to take full advantage of the next financial crisis.

The financial world, and possibly the US currency, will experience a trust crisis which will cause a transfer of wealth away from highly indebted and leveraged banks to the safety of physical bullion held outside the banking system and outside of western jurisdictions.

Significant Milestones

Becoming a Distributor — Initial Concept Validation

Obtaining their first bullion distributorship from a Government Mint was significant because it meant that Silver Bullion was now recognised enough by industry players to warrant an official relationship. To Mr Gregersen, this, along with a healthy customer demand, meant that his business had graduated from "hobby" status to a business that warranted getting a real office and full-time employees.

Moving into Services — Going to a Global Audience

Initially, the business was to sell bullion minted from various mints and foundries around the world. The problem with this business model is that other companies can easily do the same. This will eventually result in a downward spiral of lower and lower profit margins as new competitors under-price the existing market.

Mr Gregersen does not want to be in the commodity business, which has low barriers to entry and is a transaction business with little customer loyalty because it would mean that they would have to compete primarily on price. Such a business model would also restrict the customer base to the local retail market. He wanted to do much more.

So the next logical step was to build on their commodity base and create long-term customer relationships through the storage of bullion. Because they saw real shortcomings in many competing storage offerings and because they were able to credibly solve these problems, the storage business took off, giving them global rather than local reach.

Building Our Own Vault — Removing Foreign Middlemen

Although they sell and store bullion, their business is really about the trust that a customer bestows on them and Mr Gregersen is determined to do everything to protect the customer's interests and grow this trust.

A study of Western fiscal situation, monetary policies and history will show that over the next decade there is a high chance that we will see a repeat of the 1933 US gold nationalisation during which time the United States made gold ownership illegal.

Singapore is considered one of the safest jurisdictions to protect customers from such a nationalisation event and that is the reason gold and silver is flowing into Singapore. However most vaults in Singapore are run by large global companies that are very exposed to US regulations thereby exposing a major jurisdictional flaw because they might be forced to follow US law and send bullion back to the US if a nationalisation occurs.

Hence, to ensure Silver Bullion's customer bullion cannot be easily nationalised or confiscated by foreign governments, they took the big step to build their own vault — The Safe House — to provide the best protection possible.

The Next 50 Years

The business is shaped by long-term cycles. When the US left the gold standard in 1971 this set the basis for easy credit and eventually led to a world dominated by large banks who benefited handsomely from money printing, debts and easy credit.

In the West, debts have now become so massive that the only reason our current financial system is still working is because the vast majority of people do not understand the extent of the problems, says Mr Gregersen.

Over the next decade these excesses will have to be dealt with, and most traditional financial institutions and indebted western governments will experience a massive loss of power due to past mis-management and a loss of trust by the public.

On the flip side, we will see a shift of power to the developing world and Asia and an increased demand for traditional stores of value outside the banking system such as physical gold, silver and land.

The crisis might also see the wide acceptance of crypto currencies and distributed payment systems (Internet) that can easily automate away most traditional banking services. These technologies do not require a central clearing company or exchange and, if properly understood by the masses, will be trusted and accepted.

Within this context, Silver Bullion will be a reliable store of value and will benefit immeasurably from these changes.

It is impossible to say what will happen

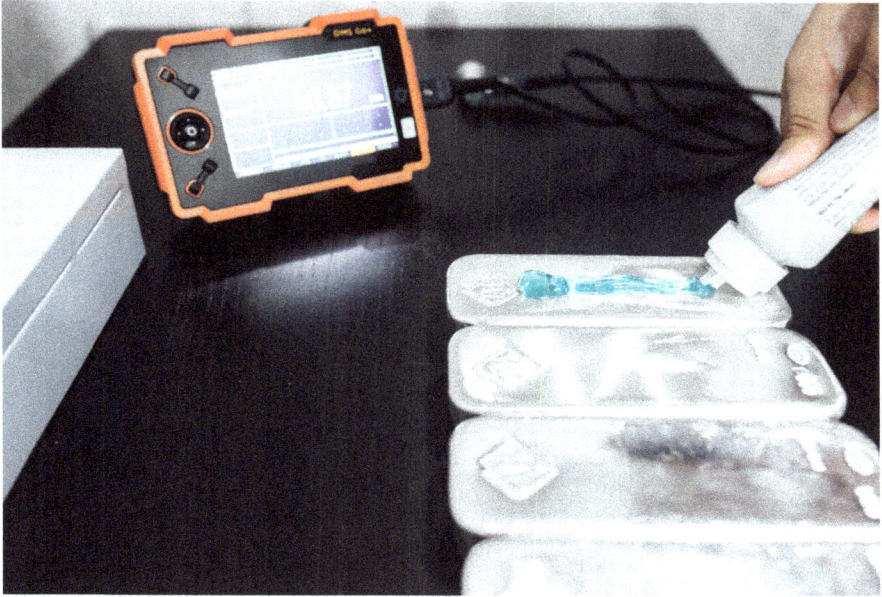

exactly but the world will always need a reliable store of value, especially in a time of crisis, and Silver Bullion will be there providing the safest place for your gold and silver.

Major Contributions to the Economy

Within the context of the Singapore economy Silver Bullion is still a minor player, so Mr Gregersen doubts they have had a major contribution in terms of numbers.

They did however play a role in Singapore's stated goal to become an internationally recognised Bullion Trading Hub and virtually created the market for Silver Bullion in Southeast Asia.

Going forward, he also believes the company will be playing a bigger role because they created the infrastructure to securely store 1.5% of globally known, above-ground silver supplies as well as considerable amounts of gold, and they have the right solution to benefit from a global crisis.

Major Influences and Inspiration

- Elon Musk. Elon will probably become the greatest entrepreneur in the history of mankind.
- Lee Kuan Yew. Mr Gregersen moved to Singapore because of his book "From Third World to First" and has been promoting Singapore to everybody he meets

because of his policies. He hopes that Lee Kuan Yew's pragmatic policies will be replicated in many countries.

- Robert Zubrin. Robert made the prospect of a colony on Mars a realistic endeavour and heavily influenced NASA's plan for Mars. More importantly, he inspired countless entrepreneurs, including Elon to make humanity a multi-planetary species.

Name a Dish that Best Represents You or Your Business

Vietnamese Pho. Mr Gregersen says he could eat it every day and, to some degree, represents his internationality.

Giving Back

Mr Gregersen believes in treating employees and customers well. The company had an opportunity to donate money for cancer research and have it matched multiple times.

However he believes that the real value of Silver Bullion is to help people, who are willing to listen, to see the bigger picture.

The world is changing and we will experience a financial earthquake whose power has been building over the last 40 years. It will affect all of us and having a rough understanding of our financial problems can be a financial lifesaver, he added.

Company Culture

Trust is the most important factor at Silver Bullion. Mr Gregersen says he can trust everybody implicitly at the company and is proud of this. Many employees also own shares, making them co-owners and giving them a stake in the company.

They have a flat hierarchy and as much as possible he likes to have people speak their minds. Culture and trust is critical. If they do not have trust within the company, how could they ask a customer to trust them with his bullion?

An Idiom to Describe Your Business

The safest place for your silver and gold.

Sing Lun Holdings

CEO: Mark LEE

"Build your team, empower them and have trust in them."

Company Profile

Sing Lun Holdings is a privately-owned enterprise with a diverse range of business interests worldwide including Industries, Investments and Real Estate.

The industrial arm holds interests in SL Global, a full-service provider of apparels, incorporating design and developmental services to manufacturing and supply chain management of a full range of apparel products covering knits, wovens and sweaters. Its manufacturing and sourcing offices are located in Singapore, Malaysia, Vietnam, Cambodia, Sri Lanka, China, and Indonesia. Customers include The North Face, Puma, Under Armour, Oakley, Brooks Running, Lucy Yogawear, SuperDry, Timberland, Nautica, Macy's Departmental Store and Osh Kosh B'gosh.

A direct investment arm holds interests in businesses that leverage on their retail supply chain and manufacturing know-how. This includes a fashion business in Korea known as Atria, that seeks to churn out fast Korean designer fashion.

Setback & Recovery

During the beginning of the financial crisis in 2008, one of Sing Lun's customers had a major management restructure. This led to a change in its strategic direction and resulted in an exit from businesses in some of the countries that Sing Lun was operating in. This exit meant the loss of 30% of Sing Lun's capacity overnight as orders retreated, forcing the closure of two of its oldest plants and the retrenchment of 600 of its loyal staff. Most of the employees had grown with Mr Mark Lee's dad, and have literally seen him grow up, from a young child to becoming CEO of the company.

They were more family than employees and breaking such difficult news was not easy. Standing in front of everyone with a microphone, and explaining the situation is a moment he will never forget. Determined to ensure that Sing Lun would never again be over-reliant on a single customer, the company now represents more than two dozen reputable apparel brands, ranging from performance sportswear, fashion wear and children's brands.

Must-have Qualities of Successful Entrepreneurs

- Always have a positive outlook and persevere through difficult moments of a crisis. This is not about blind faith, but taking a calculated position in what you believe in, and staying the course. This also means that you must always know what your worst case scenarios are for you and your company — can you and the company survive through any "knock-out" punch, or are you able to live,

stand-up and fight another day? Mr Lee always says, "We plan for the worst, but hope for the best".

- Never be complacent, even if the company is doing well. The market changes faster than we think at times, and we must constantly be paranoid about what our customer will need, and what our competitors are or will be doing. Although things might be going well at the moment, the leadership team must fearlessly drive change within the organisation to address future changes.

- Success can never be achieved by one person. It's a team effort and building and developing human capital needs to be at the forefront of any growth strategy. Build your team, empower them and have trust in them. If your phone keeps on ringing, and either your customers or staff keep calling you, then something is wrong with the organisation.

Turning Point

Within Sing Lun's apparel supply chain management services, Mr Lee began to cast a critical eye over the market needs and, in 2006, identified a growing global consumer trend in health and fitness, driven by the spending habits of a growing ageing population seeking to maintain good health. He understood immediately that he could fill a gap in the market and made the bold move to expand into the performance sportswear segment. It was a controversial decision as the firm's existing production facilities had to be re-engineered to meet the sportswear industry's standards and employees had to undergo new training.

Overcoming the initial fear and resistance, Mr Lee and his team were wholly committed to bringing about this change and, over the next few years worked tirelessly to expand its presence in this segment. Their efforts, and his decision were soon validated when the performance sportswear industry took off and the company was positioned to reap the benefits. They swiftly won over recognised brands such as Underarmour, The North Face, Puma, Timberland, Oakley and Brooks Running. In time, sportswear became the predominant category for Sing Lung and today accounts for more than 70% of the company's turnover.

Milestones

- Mr Lee's first milestone was achieved with his father and the team, taking the apparel supply chain business public in 2000 on the mainboard of the Singapore Stock Exchange. It meant working closely with the family members, key staff, and the then newly formed board of directors and members of the investment community. This really taught him how to transit from being a simple family business to a business that focused on responsible corporate governance, and incorporating best practices of transparency, corporate social responsibility and world class processes into the business. This also allowed him to learn about the capital markets, and how to effectively use them to grow and maximise shareholder's interests.
- His second milestone was transitioning the company from a family business to a business that now has professional employees in the form of a C-suite leadership team, yet also maintaining family values of respect, responsibility and long term investment horizons within business decisions. His personal view is that to take a company through to each growth milestone, S$100 million to S$300 million to S$500 million and beyond will need different management skillsets. This will mean making difficult but necessary changes to management and leadership. Unless one is resolute and determined to identify these gaps and close them, the company will stand still.
- The third milestone was the need to change the company's business to align with the mega-trends of the century within Singapore and the region. This might mean re-aligning the business portfolio, making difficult decisions like exiting a business, or a manufacturing location and even exiting from a customer relationship. The company has done all of the above in order to survive and thrive.

The Next 50 Years

It's difficult to accurately predict how the world will change over the next 10 years, and even harder to predict over 50 years! However, the principles remain the same — monitor the mega-trends, understand how they will impact your business, identify any gaps between now and the future, set a plan to close these gaps, and fearlessly drive change within your organisation to meet these changes.

It's easier said than done. However, if the culture is imbued within the organisation, and there's a paranoid sense of belief within the leadership team, then half the battle is won. The Internet is really a game-changer within the industry. It's affecting the entire supply chain, from how the consumer buys their products, which will change the tenant base of a shopping mall, to how goods will be shipped from manufacturers to customers, and how within the manufacturing process, it will need to be re-tuned to meet these individualised and even customised needs of the consumer in future.

This is a significant impact within this space and Sing Lun will be adapting its manufacturing processes to meet them. The second mega-trend will be the amalgamation of electronics to everyday clothing or wearables. Consumers will expect more functionality from their clothing and accessories, whether in areas of anti-bacteria, quick-dry, UV cut, and even monitoring their vitals. The company is investing heavily in this and innovating our products to meet these trends.

Contribution to Singapore

The industry is labour intensive. In the past, while the manufacturing facility was still in Singapore, this gave the less educated a good livelihood and enabled them to become craftsmen/women. Although they have since moved manufacturing facilities abroad, such ex-staff have managed to take on these skills to start their own small businesses in tailoring and handiwork.

They still have over 130 personnel in the Singapore office, and have since upgraded the teams here to Overseas Head-quarters Office (OHQ). They recognised that their roots are here, and continue to upgrade the team in Singapore to perform OHQ functions and roles.

Even as the business's footprint expands to more than seven countries, they continuously send the local team abroad. The ability for Singaporeans to attain cross-cultural management expertise and skills are vital to our economy. Singapore itself is a small economy, and by pushing our hinterland wider, we can give more opportunities to skilled Singaporean PMETs for a chance of a good job abroad.

Major Influence and Inspiration

Mr Lee cites his father. He's been an incredible mentor and teacher, and left big shoes to fill.

Name a Local Dish that Best Represents You or Your Business

Cantonese steamed fish. Because it takes the right temperature and timing to get the fish steamed properly. Too long, it's overcooked. Too short a time, it's too raw. The ingredients that make up the dish must be in the right proportions – not too salty, not too sweet, and with the right garnishing at the end for the ultimate presentation.

Do not take too long to adapt to market forces, because one will lose market share. Take too short a time to study the market and make a hasty decision, and you will end up with a raw deal. Sing Lun's success lies in putting the right team and structure in place. Finally, marketing is the garnishing. You must always know how to market the company to achieve a sustainable competitive advantage.

Giving Back

Sing Lun Holdings places a strong emphasis on corporate social responsibility. These initiatives are mainly driven by Mr Lee's father, Mr Patrick Lee, who continues to be the Chairman of the Group. "Our emphasis on business must be balanced by giving back to society. Today's society over-emphasises on economic success. However, we must not forget our roots, understanding our culture and helping those that have not been as fortunate as us," says Mr Patrick Lee. Sing Lun's CSR efforts are focused on aiding university students that are less fortunate and the elderly and sick as well as helping more people appreciate their heritage and culture.

This is done through a scholarship the company has endowed with Singapore Management University, as well as Mr Lee's active participation as Chairman in both

Kwong Wai Shu Hospital and Singapore Chinese Orchestra, as well as serving as Secretary General of the Singapore Federation of Chinese Clan Associations (SFCCA).

An Idiom to Describe Your Business

If change is happening faster on the outside than the inside, then the end is near. Only by recognising change and driving the business to meet these changes will we be always relevant and sustainable.

SLP International Property
Consultants Pte Ltd

CEO Kain SIM, Deputy MD Tricia TEO

"Many homegrown real estate agencies suffer a short life span due to increased competition and lack of vision and strength to remain resilient."

Company Profile

Started in 2001, SLP International started out as a boutique agency specialising in the marketing of industrial projects for SMEs in Singapore. SLP International has set itself a vision to be a home grown international agency. The agency continues to expand its business division over the years from business space projects to residential projects. It is also the first local agency to have its own research and consultancy arm headed by Mr Nicholas Mak. They have continued to expand their services and revenue base to also include property and facility management as well as International Property Marketing. Valuation will also be another service that the agency will add to eventually become a full service agency.

Extending its regional presence, the agency has established offices in Jakarta, Shanghai, Hong Kong and Malaysia. The agency currently boasts the largest full time business space team of 40 dedicated staff as well as 50 full-time staff in the residential and international property marketing industries. With a full-time staff strength of 100, the agency is Singapore's largest home grown property consultancy firm. SLP International also owns SLP Realty, a subsidiary agency that has 1000 agents to supports its residential projects.

Setbacks and Memorable Lessons

The agency business is heavily human resource intensive. The competition in the real estate sector has been intense with other companies poaching staff that SLP had taken a long time to train up. Over the years, the business has suffered from bouts of people leaving the company for greater compensation. The lessons learnt for SLP, says CEO Ms Sim, is that they must become more resilient to such a threat by developing a framework and business processes that are not easily duplicated by competitors.

Advice to Budding Entrepreneurs

The environment for entrepreneurs today is more challenging than ever before. With the advent of technology, particularly e-commerce, the opportunities are greater, but so is the competition. To thrive in such an environment, today's entrepreneur has to be more creative to stay ahead. To stay agile and nimble is also critical to ride each storm as it comes.

Must-have Qualities of Successful Entrepreneurs

- Vision and purpose. There must be a clear vision and purpose for the business. Without this it will be hard for the business to obtain sustainable success as there are always many setbacks to be faced along the way. Having a vision and purpose will help the entrepeneur to focus on his path and remain vigilant.

- Risk-taking. An entrepreneur must take calculated risks but at the same time he/she must not be easily deterred by loss or failure and must be willing to take losses as lessons for future success.
- Passion. The entrepreneur must love what they do and do what they love, which will see them through no matter what the circumstances.

Turning Point

The turning point for the business started after winning the Enterprise 50 award in 2008. Gaining recognition in the marketplace, the company was able to attract more talented professionals to join and expand its business. During the 2008 Lehman Brothers Crisis, the company lost $1 million in six months. However, the business strengthened and turned around in 2009 and continued to grow to the current day strength of about 1000 agents in SLP Realty and 100 full time staff in SLP International.

Significant Milestones

- Regional expansion and winning the Enterprise 50 awards. In 2006 PT SLP International was established in Jakarta, followed in 2009 and 2013 by three offices in Shanghai and Iskandar Malaysia. SLP International's achievement was also recognised by the winning of the Enterprise 50 award both in 2008 and 2013.

- Foray into residential project marketing. SLP's expansion into residential project marketing started to gather momentum in 2008 with the launch of Natura Loft by Qing Jian Realty. This is the first development project for Qing Jian Realty, which, prior to this, was predominantly a construction company in Singapore. In proving its commitment to the project, SLP International also took a stake in this development through its sister company ZACD Investments Pte Ltd. The project was launched a month after the Lehman Brothers financial crisis in 2008. It was a tough market. However through its aggressive and innovative marketing approach, SLP International fully sold the project.

With the success of Natura Loft, SLP International was appointed for many more residential projects by Qing Jian Realty, leading to the successful sales of RiverParc EC in Seng Kang, Flo Residence in Punggol, Ecopolitan, Waterbay, Parc Centro, Lush Acres, and Nin Residence etc. During this time, SLP has successfully made a foray into marketing residential projects focusing mainly in heartland areas such as Sengkang, Punggol and Woodlands.

- Expansion into Iskandar Malaysia. In 2013, SLP expanded its business into Iskandar Malaysia. Focusing on providing the business space solution to the many Singapore SMEs, the company led several companies into expanding and establishing business operations in the Iskandar Malaysia region. The Frontier, a detached factory project with gated swecurity by WB Land Sdn Bhd was a sell-out with several Singapore companies. Following this success, SLP International has been appointed for several other Iskandar projects namely Nusajaya Techpark, Senibong88, Empire Park and Alam Jaya Business Park.

The Next 50 Years

SLP wants to continue to build and develop the business model to be one that is viable, sustainable and relevant in the coming years. In order to achieve this, they aim to groom the next level of leadership with business acumen and an international outlook. Many homegrown real estate agencies suffer a short life span due to increased competition and lack of vision and strength to remain resilient and relevant in the industry. SLP seeks to overcome this by having a regional and international outlook as well as partnering others for success. For example, SLP is instrumental in bringing Chinese, Indonesian and Singapore companies into several joint venture developments.

Several factors influence the development of the real estate agency business. Now, we are in the digital age, and with the increased worldwide liquidity and the opening up of migration policies, there is greater demand and awareness for property investment worldwide. The business is evolving towards wealth management/investment with the increased demand in property acquisition worldwide. Training of real estate personnel in wealth management is now part and parcel of the profile. With the advent of technology, investors may reach a point where they will buy property online. Therefore, it is important to upgrade the skills of real estate agents. Many funds in the market are now actively acquiring property agencies and are gaining popularity worldwide as a form of credible brick and mortar investment. The real estate business is very much trending towards wealth and fund management.

Major Contributions to the Economy

- Helping SMEs to grow and expand through better designed factory space and relocation, and also helping SMEs to design, build and find good locations, e.g., helping companies to set up factories in Iskandar Malaysia.

- With offices in Shanghai, Hong Kong and Jakarta, SLP helps to market Singapore property in these overseas markets. At the same time, the company also trained and equipped staff to manage these overseas offices. With the increasing expansion, staff are trained to have cross-cultural exposure and an international business outlook.

- SLP markets and sells many EC projects in the heartlands. They work with developers to develop affordable and beautiful lifestyle homes for Singaporeans.

Representing Singapore Internationally

The vision and mission for SLP is to be a homegrown international name. The business started out in industrial project marketing, and through this, they are well connected with many of the SMEs in Singapore. Being a project marketing company, they work with developers to design good, functional business spaces for clients. With the greater business space efficiency and facilities, this indirectly helps clients to increase productivity and their business profile. In this regard, SLP believes they can represent Singapore on an international platform by partnering with developers overseas to design and build innovative and efficient business spaces.

Major Influence and Inspiration

The major influence and inspiration to Ms Sim from young was her father. In fact, she says, he was very much like the late Mr Lee Kuan Yew. No nonsense, strict and expecting excellence always, as well as someone who had great passion and vision in his work. He was also an entrepreneur/businessman who built a chemical business from nothing. For this reason, she read a lot about the late Mr Lee and admires his conviction, tenacity and lifework in building Singapore as a nation. He strived to give a better life and success to every citizen. SLP would like to use this platform created as a company to inspire and build success for the people who work with them.

Name a Local Dish that Best Represents You or Your Business

If Ms Sim were to think of SLP as a local dish, it would be Yong Tofu. Yong Tofu is a healthy dish that can be customised, and is innovative as you can always introduce new ingredients. It is versatile; you can have it in soup or dry. It is also easy to cook and can be adapted to be sold in another country or culture. This very much signifies SLP's spirit of being a healthy company, serving the needs of clients, being innovative and having a business model that can be replicated in other countries for expansion.

Giving Back

Ms Sim says that SLP is and has always been a strong advocate of corporate social responsibility. They believe in growing into a wholesome company where one can bring awareness and its people together to work towards a worthy cause. Generosity and giving back is an integral part of the corporate culture that they are practising.

Company Culture

SLP practices a culture of care, love and opportunity so everyone can achieve their potential. They promote an entrepreneurial spirit in the company, empower and encourage staff to think outside the norm and be innovative and be willing to take calculated risks. They want everyone to take ownership and lead. They run several CSR (corporate social responsibility) programmes to bring people together to work towards a worthy cause. One example is their yearly Christmas Tree wish list for the needy and underprivileged families where staff pick and contribute the gifts.

Spectra Innovations Pte Ltd

CEO K. N. SAHNEY

"Spend enough time planning upfront, including required skill sets, and above all ensure required Capital."

Company Profile

In the distribution business, Spectra plays the role of an aggregator between major product manufacturers and resellers across the region. We consolidate purchase orders from many resellers and distribute them to the respective resellers from our inventory procured directly from major manufacturers.

A centralised Distribution, Logistics & Finance Center in Singapore allows us to optimise costs and capitalise on economies of scale. Spectra has over 5000 resellers worldwide and carries products from global manufacturers including Apple, Intel, HP, Seagate, Hitachi, Toshiba, SanDisk and Logitech. The recent launch of our e-commerce portal, officesg.com, is a step towards furthering our value proposition of specially catering to the SME space in Singapore as a start.

Most Memorable Setbacks and Lessons Learnt

When we first opened our office in Pakistan we went overboard and shipped a large volume of products for local stocking which took us more than a year to liquidate. We should have done more research, talked to the customers and studied the consumption before taking a decision of stocking such a large volume of product.

Advice to Budding Entrepreneurs

Spend enough time planning upfront, including required skill sets, and above all, ensure required capital is available to sustain the early burn rate. 90% of good businesses fail due to insufficient capital.

Must-Have Qualities of Successful Entrepreneurs

- Ability to take calculated risk
- Keen eye for details
- Willing to hire or associate with people of better calibre than yourself

Turning Point

Our joint venture with a Fortune 500 Distributor which gave us good exposure and experience to restart our business. The experience helped us to understand the need for good systems, policies and best practices.

Significant Milestones

- Launch of Spectra Pakistan in 2006
- Enterprise 50 and SME 500 Awards in 2008
- Launch of officesg.com, our b2b e-commerce platform in 2014

The Next 50 Years?

I don't know about 50 years but in the next decade we will truly be an e-commerce product distributor across Asia with a strong services arm.

Industry Trends in The Next 50 Years

The big shift and trend is towards Mobility, Cloud and Connected devices (Internet of Things).

Major Contributions to the Economy

- Logistic and Transport Services
- Financial Services
- Non-Oil Exports

Representing Singapore Internationally

Our continued success for over 25 years is a living proof and validation of how Singapore can act as a strategic base and platform to penetrate difficult and challenging emerging markets.

Major Influence and Inspiration

Mr Lee Kuan Yew, after having learnt and read so much about him. We are fortunate to have shared the same era.

Name a Local Dish That Best Represents You or Your Business.

Satay: Patient and Persevering

Giving Back

Absolutely. It is prime responsibility of all companies to share a part of their success with the less fortunate from the larger society that we all come from.

Company Culture

Open and transparent with our people, customers and service providers. We are in a very competitive industry and it is important that the whole eco-system understands, respects and values what we do.

An Idiom to Describe Your Business

It Takes Two to Tango.

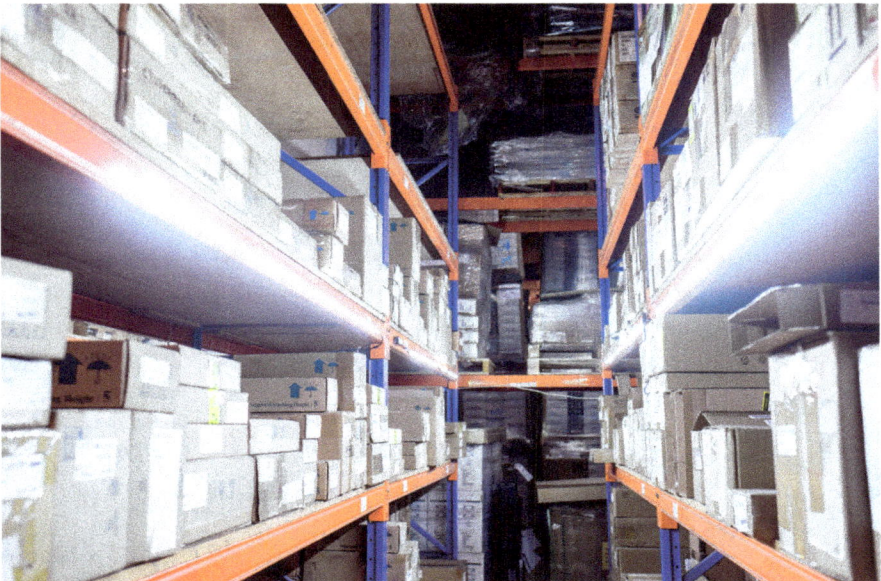

Sunray Woodcraft Construction Pte Ltd

Chairman & Founder TAN Teng Huat
Deputy Chairman & COO TAN Choon Huat
CEO Connie WU

"It seemed like a time for celebration.
However, an unfortunate accident
brought all that to an abrupt halt."

Company Profile

Sunray Woodcraft Construction Pte Ltd ("Sunray") is a Singapore-based progressive company that has business interests in commercial interior fit-out, with business activities spanning across Singapore and Southeast Asia. They have the distinction of fitting-out some of Singapore's iconic buildings, such as the two integrated resorts (Marina Bay Sands and Resorts World @ Sentosa), Shangri-la Hotel, Pan Pacific Hotel, Capitol Tower, Chijmes and National Heart Centre, to name a few. Their portfolio is diverse; encompassing office, institutional, healthcare, retail/commercial, restaurants, heritage buildings and even museums.

The Journey

Since its inception in 1987, Sunray started out as a carpentry and joinery work firm with less than 10 employees on its payroll. The current CEO of Sunray, Ms Connie Wu, worked together with Mr Tan Teng Huat, Chairman and Founder as well as Mr Tan Choon Huat, Deputy Chairman and COO. Needless to say, their journey was like any other business, filled with setbacks from time to time. Despite the odds, the pioneer generation set their mind to work doubly hard to prove their capabilities.

They threw themselves into building the business, pushing their limits day and night, and together pored over training manuals and contracts. After years of relentless hard work and effort, Sunray successfully expanded and now resides in a two-storey factory in Bukit Batok Industrial Park.

Everything was going well and it seemed like a time for celebration. However, an unfortunate and accidental fire in 1999 brought all that positive trajectory to an abrupt halt. The magnitude of the accident crippled the company's core production arm and completely ruined the head-quarter office. With insufficient insurance payout, Sunray was forced to enter into "survival mode", actively seeking help from its long-term business partners and extended family members.

"Tough times don't last, but tough people do" — this axiom proved apt for Sunray. Through support from strong familial ties and a burning desire to rebuild the company, the founders and their employees endured difficult times and only got through with sheer resilience and determination. Despite such tough times, what was especially notable was that no employees left the business and none were made to leave. These employees are dear to the hearts of the founders. Till today, each of them is still part of a big family, whether still with or no longer working in the company.

Must-have Qualities of Successful Entrepreneurs

CEO Ms Wu emphasises the importance of hard work, innovation and courage. She believes in always possessing the courage to try, having the correct attitude of persevering and also constantly thinking out of the box.

Significant Milestones

In 2015, Sunray now proudly resides in its new Sungei Kadut headquarters, a spacious complex spanning 181,000 square feet that is eight storeys high, comprising of a showroom, wood and metal production facilities, a canteen, a warehouse, a worker's dormitory, offices and a level for staff recreation. With strong emphasis on quality, timely completion and service delivery, Sunray achieved an annual revenue exceeding $200 million. The competencies of its 1500 employees across 10 countries enabled Sunray to gain recognition among industrial players and receive numerous accolades. Some of these awards include Singapore Business Superbrands, SME One Asia Award, BEI Asia Award, Singapore Prestige Brand Award and last but not least, the Enterprise 50 (E50) Awards which recognise the top 50 Small and Medium Enterprises in Singapore. To date, Sunray has successfully secured and completed many renowned local projects. In 2008, they clinched the renowned Integrated Resorts projects in Marina Bay Sands and Resorts World Sentosa. In subsequent years, Sunray participated in other iconic projects, such as TANGS, the National Art Gallery (previously Singapore's Supreme Court), Asian Civilisation Museum, and Capitol building as the most recent ones. In addition, Sunray is actively pursuing projects in ASEAN, China and the Middle East.

The Future

Strong identity; ambitious vision; determination; traditional corporate culture; prudence; caution; sustainable working relationships — these are the values that keep Sunray well poised for spectacular achievements on the global stage.

Domestically, Sunray's achievements were lauded when it clinched second place in its maiden entry to the Enterprise 50 Awards in 2014. With future overseas expansion plans on the cards, Sunray's growth potential is set in stone. Ultimately, at the heart of Sunray remains a family business with close-knit ties between employees. The future looks as apt as its name — bright and overarching. It is set to become a company not just successful in raking in the dollars and cents, but also a family MNC at heart.

Representing Singapore Internationally

Sunray aims to explore new markets and consolidate existing ones whilst adapting to change. In this pursuit, it is currently venturing into new opportunities in Malaysia, Indonesia, Thailand, Myanmar, Macau and China.

Giving Back

Sunray strongly believes in giving back to the community. One of the initiatives involves the donation of recycled paper, plastic bottles and cans to Tzu Chi Foundation Singapore. The funds collected were then used towards improving the lives of the underprivileged. Through this holistic approach, Sunray aims to be

both environmentally and socially responsible. The company also conducts charity events bi-annually involving the participation of all staff as a form of encouragement to give back to society. Some recent programmes are:

- Visiting Red Cross Home for the Severely Disabled in Dec 2014.
- In June 2015, a partnership with NUS Student Volunteers' programme known as "Paint-A-Home XVI"; which involved painting and creating a better home environment for the needy staying in one-room flats.

Company Culture

Sunray is a home grown company with a strong emphasis on a family-like culture. In the midst of the company's expansion and corporatisation, the management continues efforts in maintaining bonds. The management emphasises the importance of experiencing groundwork with the team, thus allowing better understanding between workers and staff. Their approachability and openness to discussion with all staff has subsequently translated into good relations between employees and employers. The family-like culture thus promotes open communication and teamwork — integral for project execution — between management and staff, and amongst staff themselves. In fact, the company aspires to be a "Family-MNC (FMNC)", which involves retaining the family-like culture in the process of corporatising. Such a culture brings people together not just through a corporate structure, but also through bonds. By going beyond just a typical working relationship, the culture created is conducive for all.

Major Influence

Mr Lee Kuan Yew, who dedicated his life to build Singapore. Despite the trying times, he did not give up but rose stronger. Ms Wu drew inspiration from his story and legacy.

The fire incident was devastating to the management team and it was through that event that the value of perseverance was emulated. It served as a reminder not to give up during difficult times. Sunray eventually created a miracle and success story.

Name a Local Dish that Best Represents You or Your Business

The dish that best represents Sunray is Yusheng. It may not be a local dish, but has gradually become a traditional dish, one that is not missed by Singaporeans during Chinese New Year. The different ingredients of Yusheng share similarities with Sunray, in terms of the mix of people that makes up the Sunray team.

Despite the differences, everything can be mixed seamlessly into one. In the case of the Yusheng, the mix of the different ingredients creates a refreshing and delicious dish, and in the case of Sunray, a team of people of different backgrounds and nationalities working together coherently and delivering successful projects at the end of the day.

"It is important to have a good strategy in place and more importantly, flawless execution."

Supreme Components International Pte Ltd

CEO: Vick AGGARWALA

Company Profile

Supreme Components Intl. Pte Ltd (SCI) is a leading franchised distributor of hi-tech electronic components as well as LED lighting. LED is a fast emerging technology with tremendous growth potential. Customers are changing their existing conventional lights to LED as it enables them to get savings of up to 80% on their electricity bills and maintenance costs.

SCI represents more than 50 reputable brands from Japan, Korea, Germany, UK, USA, Taiwan, China and also has offices in India and Thailand, apart from the Corporate HQ in Singapore.

SCI prides itself as being quick and agile to support customers' requests for technical support and quotations. It also has employees from ten different countries who speak 12 different languages, enabling them to have a unique understanding of the culture and nuances of doing business in each country.

Setback

During the initial phase of SCI's growth, it had purchased components from an unaudited supplier that subsequently resulted in a major malfunction and a substantial loss to the company in terms of business. More significantly, it resulted in the loss of a key customer who accounted for 75% of the company's total business and was a major hit to its reputation in the market.

The problem was eventually resolved by refunding the loss to the customer. From then on, SCI purchases products only from authorised sources that have been audited and approved by the top management.

Advice to Budding Entrepreneurs

- It is important to have a good strategy in place and more importantly, flawless execution of the strategy. STRATEGY = EXECUTION.
- One must be risk-averse. Necessary guidelines must be in place in order to mitigate the risks. Never test the depth of the river with both feet.
- Products have a short life cycle. When a product is selling well one must look to invest in R&D, in parallel, in order to come up with new products. Continual development is vital to maintain growth.

Must-have Qualities of Successful Entrepreneurs

- Perseverance
- Integrity
- Visionary

Turning Point

SCI initially started off as a trading company. They bought components from other distributors and sold them on to customers. In this way the business was very transactional and there was no security or continuity. Quality and the margins were lower.

SCI changed the model to be a franchised distributor. With this model, SCI signs a franchise agreement to represent a manufacturer in a few countries. SCI then trains the clients' engineers to provide technical support to potential customers in the design of new products.

Significant Milestones

Identifying LED Lighting as a major product that will have significant growth in the market place was important. SCI approached one of the leading manufacturers of LED in the World — CITIZEN, Japan — and got a franchise to represent them exclusively in Australia, New Zealand, Southeast Asia and India. This has proven today to be a major source of revenue for the company. Now, SCI supports the customers with LED, optics, drivers and heat sinks to build LED luminaire.

The company has also developed a virtual office concept. Sales professionals from many countries who understand the respective customs and culture are based in Singapore. They would then contact their respective countries and develop the market for the products represented by SCI. In this way. SCI saves cost in maintaining a separate office in each country. Sales professionals also leverage on the corporate facilities like accounting, HR, and warehouse facilities. They can also be easily guided and supervised by the top management on a day to day basis.

The joining of Mr Piyush Aggarwala (Son of the CEO), who had spent 13 years in USA studying and working for an IT consulting company, has also brought in new impetus into the business. He has significantly improved the web site of SCI, attracting more visitors and providing more targeted information to potential customers. He has also brought in fresh ideas on improving the Operational aspects of SCI's business.

The Future

SCI expects to diversify into clean energy and energy efficiency. A more long term goal is to be its own manufacturer of finished products resulting in vertical integration. Aspirations are high and the vision translates into becoming a truly global company with a footprint in all the major countries.

Major Contributions to the Economy

- Providing employment to Singaporeans
- SCI is ranked as Top 50 in terms of overseas revenue
- SCI has engaged many other local vendors, e.g. freight forwarders, bankers

Representing Singapore Internationally

SCI will continue to open many branch offices in other countries, while providing quality products and services. In turn, this will reinforce the image of Singapore as a place for quality companies and quality service providers.

Major Influences

- Robert G. Miller, Chairman and CEO of Future electronics (a multi-billionaire) on business
- Jack Welch on Leadership

Name a Local Dish that Best Represents You or Your Business.

Being a vegetarian, Mr Aggarwala likes spinach soup served in a bamboo cup at the award winning Ling Zhi Vegetarian restaurant.

Being a vegetarian is in line with his philosophy to not do harm to other living beings in the world.

Giving Back

Absolutely Yes. What goes around comes around. (e.g. we just donated tens of thousands of dollars to the 'Children's Aid Society' in Singapore)

Company Culture

Mr Aggarwala places great emphasis on culture and insists on his people living by three mantras:

Punctuality, Speed of execution and self-discipline.

"Crises are also opportunities as weaker and poorly managed companies will exit the market."

Company Profile

Tat Hong Holdings Ltd (Tat Hong) was established in Singapore in the 1970s as a supplier of cranes and heavy equipment. The company was listed on the Singapore Stock Exchange in June 2000 and is today the largest crane rental company in the Asia-Pacific region with a fleet size of more than 1500 crawler, mobile and tower cranes.

In Asia, Tat Hong has successfully leveraged its extensive crane fleet and vast experience in providing lifting solutions to establish itself as the leading name in the crane rental, heavy lift, heavy haulage and equipment sales business.

Through its wholly-owned Australian subsidiary, Tutt Bryant Group Limited, Tat Hong has a leading position in the Australian market in the areas of crane hire and heavy haulage, equipment sales and distribution and general plant and equipment hire.

Tat Hong has also expanded aggressively in China and is one of the largest tower crane rental companies in the country.

Advice to Budding Entrepreneurs

There are always ups and downs in any business — this is unavoidable. The important thing to note is that bad times will always pass and good times will not last. Therefore, we should not be discouraged when business takes a dip. When business is roaring, we should be consciously preparing for the proverbial rainy day.

Crises are also opportunities as weaker companies will exit the market while those that survive would have learnt valuable lessons and would be stronger and the better for it.

Mr Roland Ng thinks the key to being a successful entrepreneur is courage, resourcefulness, and having the "X" factor, which is the ability to source out good business opportunities which others cannot see as well as the ability to seek out talented people to work for you. Good businesses need good people.

Turning Point and Significant Milestones

The big turning point for Tat Hong was their listing, says Mr Ng. While they had to depend on their own internal resources and small bank loans previously, being a publicly listed company gave them access to more funding options and this has really helped Tat Hong to grow in the past 15 years or so.

An important milestone was the pivotal change of the business from a pure trading and distribution model to one that is increasingly focused on the rental of

cranes. Today, its crawler crane and tower crane rental businesses account for more than 55% of Tat Hong's revenue.

The second important milestone was the internationalisation of the business, which was achieved in the late 1980's through mergers and acquisitions that allowed Tat Hong to gain a foothold in the Australian market. After this, they expanded into the region and then China.

Last but not least, was the professionalising of the business through constant improvement of services and safety standards.

The Next 50 Years

Tat Hong is already the largest crawler crane owner and rental company in the Asia Pacific region but there is still room to continue to grow and expand the footprint. Right now, they have a presence in Singapore, Malaysia, Thailand, Vietnam, Indonesia, China, Australia and Papua New Guinea and there are many large markets which have yet to be tapped into. Mr Ng says the company will start to make inroads into these markets and make Tat Hong a dominant and reputable crane rental company in this part of the world.

Looking beyond, there is a huge infrastructure deficit in Asia and this will be remedied in the years to come — power generation, airports, ports, railroads, etc.

There is also the urbanisation of populations which leads to a requirement for housing, clean water, roads, etc. In addition, China has announced plans for "一带一路" which includes the Maritime Silk Route, and if this is undertaken, it will spur vast infrastructure development in the countries from China, through Southeast Asia to Europe and Africa.

Contributions to Singapore

Tat Hong's first contributions were in the industrialisation of Singapore. When Singapore started to industrialise, Tat Hong was among the first companies to supply the heavy equipment required to build the JTC factories and other buildings. Following this was the urbanisation and finally, the modernisation of Singapore. All through the building of modern Singapore, Tat Hong's cranes have been involved. From HDB flats, schools, universities, hospitals and factories to petrochemical plants on Jurong Island, Changi Airport and MRT stations, their cranes were involved in building the foundations of modern Singapore.

The Tat Hong name is synonymous with cranes. As the largest crane rental company in the Asia-Pacific region, it already represents Singapore in the crane rental space in many countries in the region, with its operations in China, Hong Kong, Australia, Malaysia, Thailand, Indonesia, Vietnam and Papua New Guinea.

Major Influence and Inspiration

Mr Ng pays tribute to his father and his astuteness in business. He had a battery and tire shop in the 1960's and way back then, he had the foresight to see that heavy equipment would be required in the building of Singapore and he started importing construction equipment, literally one piece at a time from Japan. This was how Tat Hong began.

Name a Local Dish that Best Represents You or Your Business

Instead of food, Mr Ng thinks Chinese tea represents his business. Although this drink may taste quite bland, it is highly appreciated. At all Chinese banquets, you will find Chinese tea being served even though it is not the highlight of the meal.

This is the same for Tat Hong's cranes — you will find cranes at all construction sites even though they may not be the centre of attraction. Unobtrusive as it is, the crane makes its presence felt because building and construction work will grind to a halt if it is not around to do the lifting.

Giving Back

As a corporate citizen, Tat Hong conducts its business responsibly and part of that responsibility dictates that one has to take care of the society and the environment in which one operates. The Tat Hong Group has a long-standing tradition of caring for the community. Their corporate philanthropic efforts support a variety of causes to benefit wide-ranging members of the community who need assistance through donations and sponsorships.

In addition, in Singapore, they sponsor the "Free Groceries" CSR project where twice a year, they provide free groceries to needy residents in rental flats in Toa Payoh. For this project, Tat Hong sponsors the grocery items whilst its staff volunteer their time and assist these needy families.

Culture as a Key Ingredient in Success

Tat Hong grew from a family business and whilst they have embraced modern technology and business processes, the philosophy that employees are part of the family has not changed. Mr Ng believes employees also feel a certain attachment to the company, which is why there have been many cases of employees' children who followed their parents' footsteps and worked for Tat Hong.

An Idiom to Describe Your Business

A Chinese idiom comes to mind and that is 顶天立地. This is because cranes are used everywhere from the ground where you can find Tat Hong's crawler and mobile cranes and in the sky where their tower cranes are found. Tat Hong's cranes are involved in every stage of construction, from ground preparation right through to the completion of the building work, and are often among the first equipment to arrive at the site and the last to leave.

"People always ask me what makes TYJ successful. I tell them it's because of the 3 "S"s: Start Small, Be Specialised, Develop a Strong Brand."

Tee Yih Jia Group

Exec Chairman: Sam GOI

Company Profile

Tee Yih Jia (TYJ) is a global food manufacturer with operations in Singapore, Malaysia, USA, Europe and China. As the largest spring roll pastry manufacturer in the world with a production capacity of 35 million pieces a day, it exports its Asian food products, which include a wide variety of ready-to-eat Asian convenience foods such as spring rolls, roti paratha, crepes, mini prawn rolls, glutinous rice balls and samosas to over 100 countries including North America, Europe, Russia, the Middle East, Australia, China, Japan and the rest of Asia Pacific. TYJ was awarded first place among Singapore's 50 best companies at the Enterprise 50 Awards in 2000.

In addition, Mr Goi is the Executive Chairman of GSH Corporation Limited, a growing property developer in China and Southeast Asia. GSH Corporation, which owns and operates the Five-Star Sutera Harbour Resort, marina and golf course in Kota Kinabalu, has prime properties currently under development in Singapore and Malaysia. He also has investments across a range of listed and private entities in numerous industries, such as food and beverage, consumer essentials, recycling, distribution and logistics.

Memorable Setback and the Lessons Learnt

TYJ embarked on a large scale automation drive very early on. This changed the shape of our popiah skins from round to square. Our new popiah skins were initially rejected by the then master chefs who were set in their cooking methods and accustomed to the round pastry. I believed in my product and campaigned to break the pre-conceived mindset that square pastries were inferior, and showed them how it was just as good if not better.

The main lesson I got out of this experience was that even if you have a superior product, it doesn't mean people or the industry will readily accept it. Entrepreneurs have to believe in the value of their products and be confident enough to fight for it, and never take no for an answer.

Advice to Budding Entrepreneurs

I am extremely hardworking and unyielding. I had an innate ability to understand what would drive people and bring them together. Today, these traits alone may not have gotten me so far.

These fundamental traits of an entrepreneur will always remain prerequisites to success. However, today, entrepreneurs have to also be highly sophisticated, technologically-skilled and media-savvy. They have to deal with customers having access to information on demand and a choice to work with many other parties globally, not just locally. The main thing entrepreneurs must think about today is to go global from day one.

Entrepreneurs must know every aspect of their business. TYJ is in the business of frozen food; we export 90% of our products to the world. I had to learn best practices in food safety and quality standards from other developed countries to make the best product, but it didn't stop there. I had to understand sales, marketing, human resource, accounting and everything in between.

Another aspect of being an entrepreneur which sets us apart is that we are able

to embrace opportunities and take calculated risks in our businesses and work hard to make the opportunity a success. TYJ's expansion has created a global footprint for the Group today. We undertook growth through strategic acquisitions and organic expansions, integration and embraced innovation.

My business interests cover F&B, property, technology, environment and healthcare. As you build your business, you require a capable team to execute your vision. The emerging generation of entrepreneurs will have their way of doing things as they will understand today's consumers best. My priority now is to mentor them, put in place a leadership team to take the company forward.

Must-have Qualities of Successful Entrepreneurs

People always ask me what makes TYJ successful. I tell them it's because of 3 "S"s. Firstly, we started small — being nimble, we managed to gain a foothold in a competitive market. Being small, we were also specialised and we played out niche advantage to the maximum. And by being specialised, we have built a strong brand equity. These have been our success factors.

Turning Point

Our automation drive in the early 1980s was one of the pivotal moments for the business. This turned a small factory supplying popiah skins to a tiny domestic market into one that had the scope to supply popiah skin to every household in the world.

The automation drive made TYJ compliant with global standards, which paved the way for us to work with international firms to design and build our unique machinery.

This put us on our way to success, and we never looked back. We constantly aspired to achieve higher standards, greater productivity and become better at what we did.

Significant Milestones

- The first was our automation drive in the early 1980s.
- Next, between the 80s and 90s, we looked to expand our footprint and to lower our costs. Through a combination of organic expansion and strategic acquisitions, we were able to grow our business. Locally, we shifted to a larger factory and moved some of our operations to Malaysia. We expanded into Australia which went on to serve as a springboard for our internationalisation. In China, I returned to tap on the enormous marketplace and available labour.

- In recent years I have been investing in quality F&B companies to create a diversified holding and open new avenues of businesses for TYJ.

The Next 50 Years

In 50 years Singapore evolved from a third-world to a first-world nation. There were turbulent times and we survived great hardships. But with the visionary leadership of Mr Lee Kuan Yew and his team, this little red dot became a world-renowned global city we are proud of.

It is hard to say what will happen in the next 10 years, let alone 50 years. If you had asked me this question in 1977, I would never have dreamt of the extent of success TYJ would achieve.

What I can say is that TYJ will not be managed by me in 50 years. I have to find capable and quality successors to replace me and the older generation at the company. It is important that the company continues to grow from strength to strength and one day achieve the target I first set out with when I took over TYJ — for its product to be in every household in the world.

Industry Trends in the Next 50 Years

Firstly, consumers are becoming more discerning and health conscious with regards to food. It is no longer a means simply to satisfy hunger. People want to enjoy food now, and they also want variety and to try new things. Their palates are always changing and we have to stay relevant.

The other thing we have to be conscious about is the quality and safety standards of our food. There have been many food safety scares in developing and developed nations. We have to ensure our reputation is preserved by maintaining quality checks and ensuring adherence to safety policies.

As the global population grows, producing sufficient quality food will become a challenge. This is the larger picture we have to keep at the back of our minds — feeding the world. I believe innovation and creativity will play a vital role going forward.

Major Contributions to the Economy

- TYJ is a fair employer and provides quality training for our staff.
- We export 90% of our products and promote the made-in-Singapore brand.
- From day one since I took over the business in 1977, we have strived to increase productivity and be innovative by investing in R&D.

Representing Singapore Internationally

With operations in Malaysia, USA, Europe and China, we have exported Singapore's brand of innovation and business productivity to these regions. Our products are sold in over 100 countries including North America, Europe, Russia, Middle East, Australia, China, Japan and the rest of Asia Pacific.

I believe TYJ has represented Singapore well on the international platform. We have brought the humble popiah skin and frozen products to the international marketplace and have been awarded certification by numerous national and international food safety organisations.

In my capacity as a businessman, I have taken up posts to boost bilateral relations with China, serve in various business associations and am more than willing to mentor budding entrepreneurs.

Major Influence and Inspiration

My father had a strong influence in my life. He was a hardworking man who provided for his family. He was also a businessman, and was one of the reasons I wanted to be a businessman. Even in his old age he was always the first one to come to work and the last one to leave at the end of the day. He would ensure that all the lights were switched off at the office and made sure the staff was well provided for. He never forgot his roots, and this kept me grounded.

Name a Local Dish that Best Represents You or Your Business

This will have to be the popiah. In the spirit of SG50, I would like to serve a popiah of national proportions to the people of Singapore. Here are my ingredients for the SG50 Popiah: A generous portion of confidence balanced with gratitude; a healthy measure of optimism; a teaspoon of caution; and a great deal of derring-do. And the popiah skin will be the love of our land. Now wrap it all up and flavour it to your own taste.

Giving Back

Those who are better off financially should help those who have been marginalised as both of them may be able to attribute their circumstances to the environment around them.

Philanthropy is not just all about money. In fact, it is easier to give money than to give one's time and experience in some instances. How the money is used to bring in sustainable benefits for the beneficiary and the society is more important. I work with many trade and industry associations such as International Trade Committee of the Singapore Chinese Chamber of Commerce & Industry and the Food Manufacturing Working Group to offer advice, impart knowledge and connect people. In particular, I treasure my social work with the Ulu Pandan Citizens' Consultative Committee where I raised over S$4.5 million to build a Community Centre and also spent time meeting residents from all walks of life, and who face various challenges, circumstances and hardships, especially by the low-income group who get left behind in society sometimes.

I am able to help them by listening to their problems and understanding their situations, and directing them to the right channels to receive help. When they return to thank us for our help in turning their situation around, I feel a profound sense of satisfaction that my work has made a difference in someone's life. This experience is not something money can buy.

I also believe education is a good social leveller. I am particularly fond of my work with Dunman High School Advisory and SUTD in championing the education cause. I owe my successes to my parents, my family and the community my businesses operated and grew in. In order to give back, I try to take an active role contributing to education, culture and to the less fortunate.

In 2013, I was the Fundraising Chairman for SUTD and raised more than S$110 million as part of celebrating Singapore's founding Prime Minister Mr Lee Kuan Yew's 90th birthday. Through the years I have personally donated more than S$20 million to various social, charitable and educational causes in Singapore and more than S$10 million to my hometown Fuqing and S$5 million to the Sichuan Earthquake Relief Fund.

Company Culture

TYJ has a culture of innovation and excellence. Every employee takes prides in maintaining stringent standards of food hygiene and safety, as well as utmost business ethics and professionalism.

An Idiom to Describe Your Business

"天时地利人合": I am lucky to be at the right place, doing the right things, and having the right team of people with me.

"No business is smooth-sailing. Continuously remind yourself of your passion, your aims and your goals, and nothing should daunt you."

Company Profile

Eurokars Group holds dealership rights to various renowned motor brands such as Porsche, MINI, Rolls-Royce, McLaren as well as the distribution rights to Mazda in Singapore. While its focus so far has been on the Singapore market, Eurokars has since expanded to markets in Indonesia, China and Australia.

In Indonesia, they manage Porsche, Rolls-Royce, Maserati and BMW in Western Jakarta, Mazda in South and North Jakarta, as well as the distribution of 3M vehicle-related products. Eurokars also acquired a stake in a Rolls-Royce dealership in Nanning, China in 2013.

Recently, Eurokars has established a presence in Surabaya for Porsche, Rolls-Royce and Mazda. Brands like BMW, BMW M and Maserati are also in the pipeline.

Eurokars has its sights set on becoming a leading regional dealership.

Setbacks

A setback that founder Mr Kwee had to face was trying to secure loans for the Porsche franchise in Singapore. Eurokars took over from the previous importer in 1985 who had existing business difficulties and to add to that, the economy at that time was bad. Kwee had to ovecome various obstacles to get the necessary loans from the banks.

Admittedly, it was not an easy feat, but he lets on that a lesson he picked up from this experience was the importance of perseverance. What motivated him to push through the tough times was his passion for cars, especially Porsches.

His admiration for the Porsche brand was first sparked when he saw a green Targa speed past Paya Lebar Airport in the 1970s. This was the turning point that got Mr Kwee interested in a car dealership. His experience with obstacles led him to appreciate that every problem has a solution, and one should never let a setback define his potential. Rather, perseverance and passion will help one pull through even the worst of troubles.

Advice to Budding Entrepreneurs

Have a passion in your field of work.

From past experiences, Mr Kwee strongly believes that if you have a passion for something, that would become the light that will guide you when you encounter darker times.

No business is smooth-sailing. Continuously remind yourself of your passion, your aims and your goals, and nothing should daunt you.

Aside from determination, the next most important thing would be to be firm

and confident of your decisions. However, at the same time, do not be afraid to bend a little to accommodate a particular situation. Being too rigid can backfire at times.

Significant Milestones

Entrepreneur of the Year 2006, the take-over of Mazda Singapore's distributorship in 2011 and the expansion of the car business internationally.

The Next 50 Years

In the next 50 years, Mr Kwee hopes to be able to pass down his legacy to both his son and daughter. When the time comes, he hopes his children will be able to carry on the business and build upon its success.

Looking beyond, Singaporeans are also becoming increasingly affluent and discerning about the quality and value of their cars. Much as we strive to build a world-class public transport system, there will always be Singaporeans who prefer, and can afford to, travel in a vehicle of their own.

While this means that Eurokar's target audience will only grow, they cannot become complacent and neither will their competitors. Mr Kwee foresees dealerships in Singapore becoming increasingly competitive in their sales tactics and service standards.

Eurokar's formula for success is putting the customers first and this is where it has the advantage in its long-held tradition of customer satisfaction.

Major Contributions to the Economy

Eurokars has always been a pioneering innovator with a customer-centric focus and exclusive programmes. One example of how they have transformed the industry in Singapore is in the way they pioneered organising drive clinics in Singapore in the 1980s.

Eurokars' constant support of community causes has also borne fruits for Singapore's economy. Through their long-term involvement in the Straits Times' School Pocket Money Fund, for example, they have chipped in to ensure that every Singaporean is able to achieve a respectable standard of living as the country's economy blossoms. This serves to help the economy along as society progresses. We are only truly as rich as the poorest Singaporean and Eurokars has played its part in reaching out and supporting them.

Through the recent expansion into the regional market, Eurokars has also helped to enhance Singapore's reputation as the hub from which any company looking to break into the Southeast Asian region should work from. The transparent and sincere manner in which they conduct business dealings are also reflective of the Singaporean mentality and has opened the door for business partners and their associates to work more closely with other Singaporeans.

Representing Singapore Internationally

Eurokars has grown from a small operation run with a staff of only 20 to a promising, up-and-coming SME stretching its wings in the regional market with a growing staff strength of 1200 people. Throughout the region, their approach in every market is consistent — a commitment to excellent customer service. At the same time, they always tailor their approach and responses to the unique circumstances and cultures they are working with. In this way, they believe they fly the Singapore flag high on the international stage by reflecting the excellence, efficiency and adaptability that are key traits of the success and rapid growth of both Eurokars and the nation.

Name a Local Dish that Best Represents You or Your Business

Yusheng. Similar to the salad dish which consists of different types of food and savoury delicacies, Eurokars is a dealer of various car brands ranging from premium to family brands.

Yusheng is a Teochew-style raw fish salad and consists of strips of raw fish (most commonly salmon), mixed with shredded vegetables and a variety of sauces and condiments, among other ingredients. It is enjoyed during the celebration of Chinese New Year and considered a symbol of abundance, prosperity and vigour.

However, when mixed together, it creates a whole new extraordinary and distinct flavour. For Eurokars, they have both continental and Japanese brands and convey the same high-quality standard in service throughout all their brands so that customers enjoy the "taste" of Eurokars together with the quality of the car brand that they are purchasing.

Company Culture

From their first day, every employee at Eurokars is exposed to the key ethos at the company — the customer is king. Eurokars views customer satisfaction as the key indicator of success. If a customer walks away satisfied, they would have sold him much more than one of the best cars in the world — they would have given him the Eurokars service experience. Through this sales philosophy, the company forms deep relationships with customers that ensures that they return when they're ready for their next purchase.

Another aspect of customer service involves after-sales follow-ups. Each car comes with a comprehensive warranty and maintenance package that ensures

Eurokars is able to provide the best care to customers' cars at no cost to them while the vehicle is still under warranty. Even after the warranty has expired, Eurokars still strives to provide the best possible value to customers and ensure customers are still satisfied with their purchase for years to come.

The culture of providing customer satisfaction has driven success at the company. The numbers speak for themselves. Customer satisfaction has been the cornerstone of success, building decade-long relationships with customers and expanding the Eurokars brand over the last 30 years.

An Idiom to Describe Your Business

"Even though the knife may be sharp, the fruit is sweet."

The sharp knife metaphorically represents the hardships and difficulties that a business bumps into, yet the end result of bearing the "fruit" of our labour is a rewarding and refreshing one.

This shows that no matter what obstacles Eurokars may face, they do their best to emerge from it toughened from the experience gained. Thus, setbacks will eventually lead to success as long as one does not give up.

Transworld Group Singapore

Chairman/CEO: Mahesh SIVASWAMY

"Nothing and no one can really predict the future."

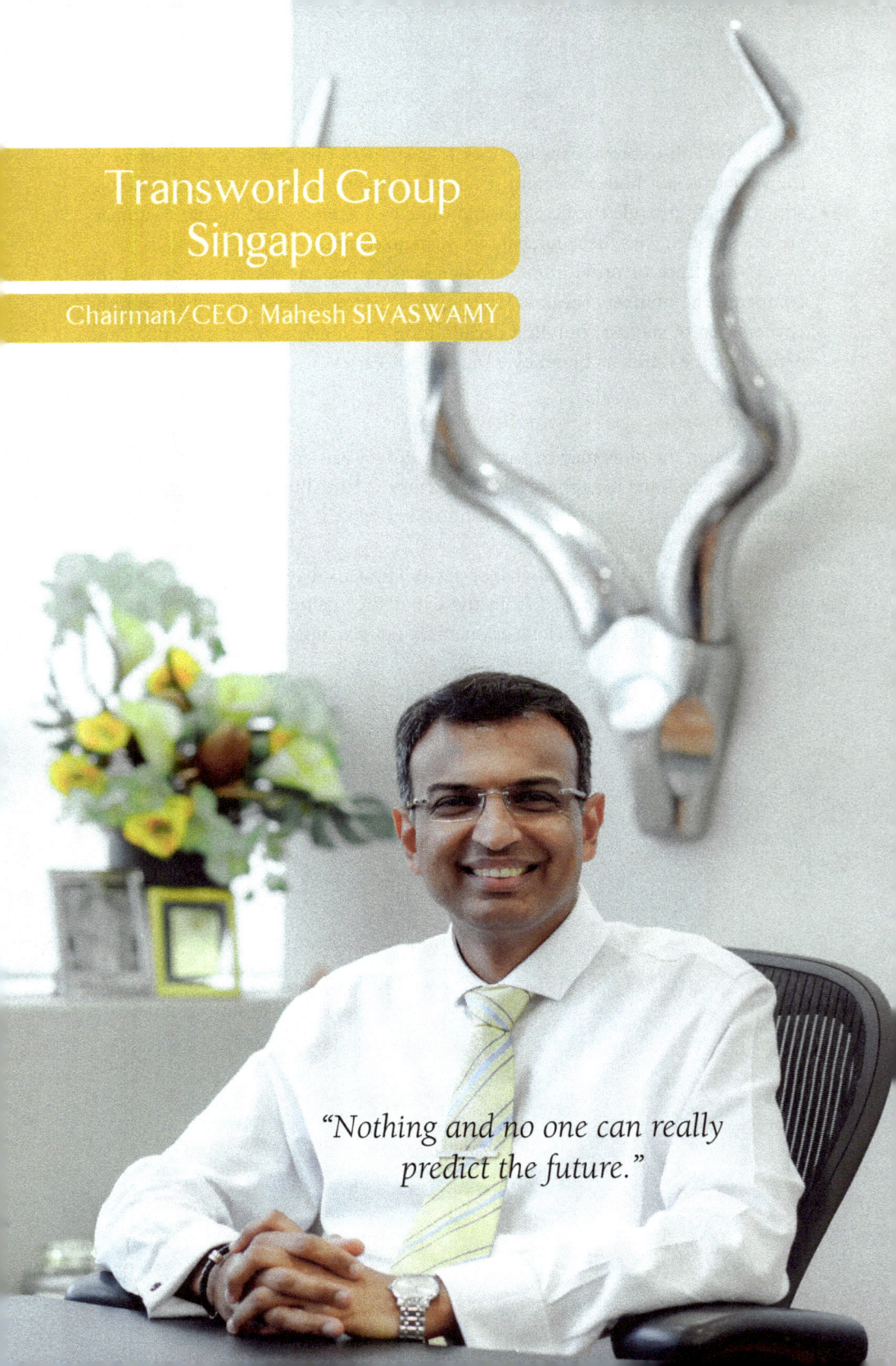

Profile

Transworld Group Singapore is one of East Asia's fastest growing shipping companies. The Group operates five subsidiaries that provide a comprehensive network of services including Ship Owning, Feeder Services, Liner Shipping, NVOCC, Logistics and Agency Representation of major shipping lines.

Services include sea freight, air freight, break bulk, land movement, warehouse logistics, projects and so on. Each subsidiary coordinates with one another to provide customised services to consumers.

A key business strength is the Group's ownership of its vessel fleet and cargo containers that ensures stability of operations. Strategically headquartered in Singapore — the world's busiest port, Transworld Group Singapore has rapidly expanded its suite of solutions. It now provides complete end-to-end shipping logistics expertise in this premier maritime hub which is connected to more than 600 ports in 120 countries around the world. At the heart of Transworld Group Singapore is a dynamic team of committed and experienced professionals that provide customised solutions for an industry that carries over 90% of the world's trade. The Group's high level of productivity is supported by fast, efficient and responsive IT systems.

Memorable Lessons

Orient Express Lines (OEL), the service division of the group, had been providing feeder container service to their biggest customer Maersk Lines out of the Malaysian port PTP for almost eight years. Around the last quarter of 2007, the top management of Maersk decided to take an active role in the Indian subcontinent. They deployed their own feeder arm on the same route that OEL were operating in, which could have resulted in huge losses of business for OEL. Almost 80% of OEL's business was dependent on just one customer and this was proving to be dangerous for the sustainability of the company. It was then that they decided to make a bold move to end the service to Maersk from PTP and decided to use PSA Singapore as a viable alternate hub port to PTP. This also helped OEL to have a bigger customer spread. They were able to provide feeder container services to a broader client base and if one customer were to go, the impact on business would not be so drastic. The main lesson learnt was to avoid over-reliance on one customer.

Advice to Budding Entrepreneurs

When you are ready to start your business:

- Focus on an opportunity that you understand well
- Don't be greedy or impatient to jump at every opportunity that you come across
- Know your own stand and situation and make a realistic plan before taking any action
- Adjust business targets based on the prevailing business trend
- Do not venture into new areas, unless your core business is stable and profitable

Turning Point

The shift from PTP Malaysia to PSA Singapore and to break away from reliance from one big customer wasn't easy. Though they provided feeder services to more customers, their ships still went light. That was when it was felt that there was a need to develop forward integration for the business. They created an NVOCC named BLPL, purchased 300 containers from the market and deployed it between Singapore and Bangladesh. Later they bought 1000 containers to make it 1300 TEUS (Twenty-foot Equivalent Units). From then on, BLPL has been growing exponentially and adding more TEUS to its fleet year on year. BLPL has added 3000 more this year, taking the total to 25,000 TEUS.

Transworld Global Logistics Solution (TGLS) had actually started as a vertical under BLPL. The purpose was to provide end-to-end logistics solutions for the customer, through sea, air and land routes. Management soon realised that they couldn't keep it that way any longer. It had reached a threshold and needed a new entity for itself. Hence TGLS was created to support the Group and develop its own business plan.

Significant Milestones

- Purchasing vessels whenever the opportunity was right without stretching their limits. Today, OEL owns six vessels (three with capacity of 1100 TEUS and 3 which are 1700 TEUS). These form a part of the owned and chartered fleet of OEL. It helps the company run an efficient container feeder service and provides a reliable service for customers.
- In BLPL, they started the reefer (temperature-controlled units) business since 2011 for perishable and frozen cargoes and have also added special equipment to handle heavy cargo to suit the individual needs of the customer. BLPI's area of operations stretches across North Asia, China, Southeast Asia, the Indian Sub-continent, Middle East and East Africa.
- In less than a year, TGLS opened their own offices in three countries — Vietnam, Thailand, and Indonesia. TGLS are now in nine countries with 36 offices and due to the cross-trade nature of business, operations extend around the globe.

The Next 50 Years

Nothing and no one can really predict the future. However Transworld Group Singapore believes that with careful succession planning and by following their vision to grow in a steady and responsible pace to a position of strength and prominence in their areas of operation, they will work towards being a strong player in the Asian markets first and then take it further ahead.

Unfortunately, the shipping industry is not currently stable and is in fact volatile. The price of bunker oil is fluctuating wildly and the charter markets, which have been steady so far, are now slowly increasing in their segments. These factors greatly affect cost of operations. On the other side, the freight rates are falling due to lack of growth in the economy and the size of the ships are getting bigger by the day. So in these scenarios, it would be difficult to comment on the trends or development for the next 50 years. However, if all the stakeholders look to operate in sensible, cost-conscious and customer-centric ways, the hope is that the industry will see some improvement in the next few years.

Major Contribution to the Economy

Shipping and logistics contributes about 8% of Singapore's GDP. As a result of the efficiency and reliability of the shipping industry, along with the incentives offered to companies across the industry, Singapore is seen as a shipping hub and a good place to do business for various related organisations like the world's top P&I clubs, financial service providers, brokers, law firms, container leasing companies etc. Therefore these factors help in the economy of the country.

Representing Singapore Internationally

Just by providing honest, credible, efficient and customer-centric service, Transworld Group Singapore aims to echo the culture and reputation that Singapore is known for. In fact, TGLS strives to become a part of the Singapore brand in their dealings worldwide. That's perhaps the reason why the group gets recognised or awarded in certain forums outside Singapore.

Major Influence and Inspiration

Mr Sivaswamy credits his father, the late Mr R. Sivaswamy (1931 – 1989).

His statement acts as a guiding light; "Action without delay is the secret of my success".

Giving Back

Transworld Group Singapore has done quite a number of charity events.
- Donations to children in Myanmar
- Typhoon Haiyan Relief Operation
- Donations to Japan Earthquake victims
- Transworld Group's Valli & Sivaswamy Memorial Charitable Trust which was formed in 1990 with a noble objective of facilitating educational, medical, and other services to the needy. E.g. Donated ambulance to a hospital in India

An Idiom to Describe Your Business

There is no short cut to success. So, keep your goals in mind and without procrastinating, work hard to achieve them.

ValueMax Group Ltd

CEO: YEAH Hiang Nam

"The business model of the pawnbroking operation has an inherent attribute of providing financial help to the community."

Company Profile

ValueMax Group Limited ("ValueMax") provides pawnbroking and secured moneylending services, as well as the retail and trading of pre-owned jewellery and gold. Having established its first pawnbroking outlet in 1988, ValueMax is one of the most established and trusted pawnbroking chains and gold traders in Singapore and has expanded to 23 outlets in Singapore at strategic locations island wide.

It has three other pawnshops operated by associate and investee companies. In Malaysia, ValueMax also operates seven outlets through its associate companies. An award-winning company, ValueMax and its subsidiaries have received various awards and certification which include (i) 15th SIAS Investors' Choice Award — Most Transparent Company Award 2014, runner up position for New Issues; (ii) 2014 Singapore SME 1000 Awards in Net Profit Excellence; (iii) 2014 Singapore SME 1000 Awards in Sales Growth Excellence; (iv) Prestige Brand Award — Established Brands 2010; (v) Enterprise 50 Award 2010; and (vi) Entrepreneur of the Year Award 2010 to its Managing Director and CEO Mr Yeah Hiang Nam. ValueMax was also the first pawnbroker to be accredited with the CaseTrust certification in 2004.

Memorable Setbacks and Lessons Learnt

In the past, the monthly held pawnbroker auctions were controlled by second hand dealers. These dealers threatened to bid for every unredeemed pledge put up for auction unless pawnbrokers paid a "protection fee" to the dealers. Bidding would generate surpluses for pawners, but meant that the auction would drag on, sometimes lasting from Saturday and overnight into Sunday. In addition, brokers would have to administer the return of the surpluses to the pawners over four months, imposing tremendous administrative work and financial costs.

When ValueMax first entered the pawnbroking business many years ago, they refused to yield to these threats nor give in to the demands of the dealers for a "protection fee". Month after month, year after year, they became the only and gradually, one of the few pawnbrokers to be "attacked" by the coalition of dealers who would bid on every unredeemed lot. For battling against the dealers and lengthening the duration of the auctions, ValueMax became unpopular at the auction sites. However, customers who received the savings passed on from earnings were appreciative and preferred to pawn at ValueMax. They recommended their friends and family and the business of ValueMax thus grew rapidly over the years.

As the Chinese saying goes, the loss of one's horse may bring fortune in the end.

Must-have Qualities of Successful Entrepreneurs

- Passion and diligence: putting the heart, mind and soul into the business
- Foresight and adaptability: ability to foresee trends and adapt to changes in the environment
- Unwavering quest towards learning and improvement.

Significant Milestones

- Listing of ValueMax, which allows the company to operate on a different platform and opens up opportunities for acquisitions.
- Exporting jewellery to overseas markets such as Dubai in the 1980s.
- Establishing production centres in Malaysia and Indonesia where production costs are cheaper and manpower is abundant.
- Establishment of ValueMax Group to consolidate subsidiary pawnshops under a holding company.

The Next 50 Years

Pawnbroking is a stable business that is anti-cyclical. There will be consolidation in this industry and ValueMax will be a major player in this consolidation process in the next 50 years. The industry is in transformation, evolving into a form of micro-finance business and may eventually provide a wider range of services. Moreover, while gold trading business volumes may fluctuate with movements in gold prices, Singapore is poised to become a regional gold trading hub and ValueMax, being one of the largest gold traders in the domestic market, will continue to serve an even more important role in the industry.

The company hopes that ValueMax Jewellery will become synonymous with pre-owned jewellery as recycling gains greater acceptance and becomes more popular. Meanwhile, the money lending business, through VM Credit, will gain a greater foothold in alternative financing.

Major Contributions to the Economy

ValueMax has changed the face of the pawnbroking business as one of the first pawnbroking chains to have modernised operations and incorporate corporate branding. They have also been a major player in the domestic gold trading business, facilitating the conversion of scrap gold into cash for pawnbrokers, jewellery retailers, dealers and jewellery factories.

They have also helped to change the concept of pre-owned jewellery by giving used jewellery a new lease of life. In-house professional cleaning, meticulous

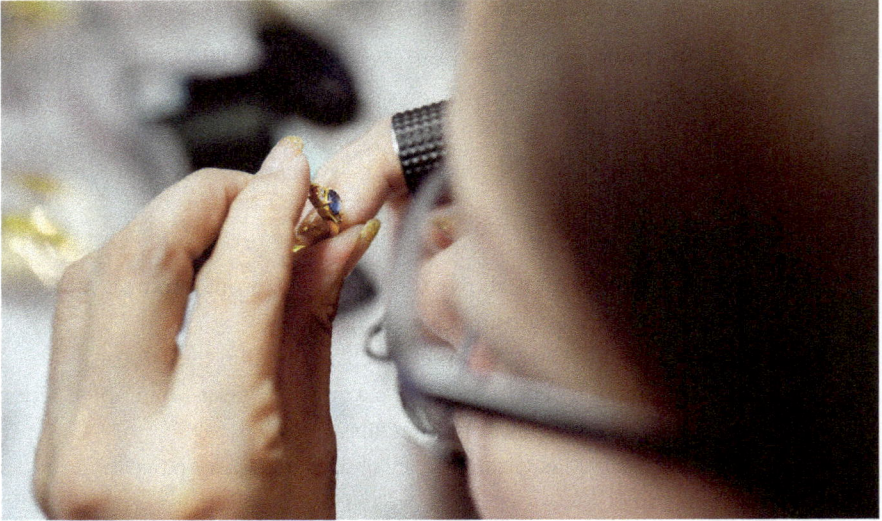

polishing and skilful reconditioning processes ensure that the pre-owned jewellery looks appealing before being displayed for sale in attractive retail settings.

ValueMax is one of the first pawnbrokers to have an overseas operation and will continue to expand overseas. It is also one of the most successfully listed pawnbrokers in Asia.

Major Influence and Inspiration

Mr Yeah points to his first boss, who operates 庸太隆 Yong Tai Long medical hall. He had great foresight and could predict economic trends with accuracy. At a young impressionable age of 17, Mr Yeah says he was fortunate to learn from him about how businesses operate in general and how international economic developments can impact on local businesses.

Name a Local Dish that Best Represents You or Your Business

Chilli crab because the corporate colour is largely red. ValueMax is fiery in their passion for the business and the business is resistant to economic fluctuations!

Giving Back

Giving back to the community can occur in various forms. The business model of the pawnbroking operation has an inherent attribute of providing financial help to the community through micro loans secured with the borrower's personal valuables. ValueMax gives the best loan-to-value ratio at a low interest rate of between 1–1.5%

a month. In case the borrower is unable to redeem the pledge, they ensure that the maximum value for the pledge will be forwarded to the borrower through the return of surpluses after auction, according to legislation. Charging thinner profit margins or using profits derived from the community to benefit that same community can generate goodwill and increase customers' interest and favourable opinions of the company.

Company Culture

A strong learning culture has been inculcated, where senior employees share knowledge and contribute to the growth and development of junior colleagues. ValueMax also has a family-like environment and every member of staff is given a budget to build better relationships with their colleagues and foster greater team cohesiveness.

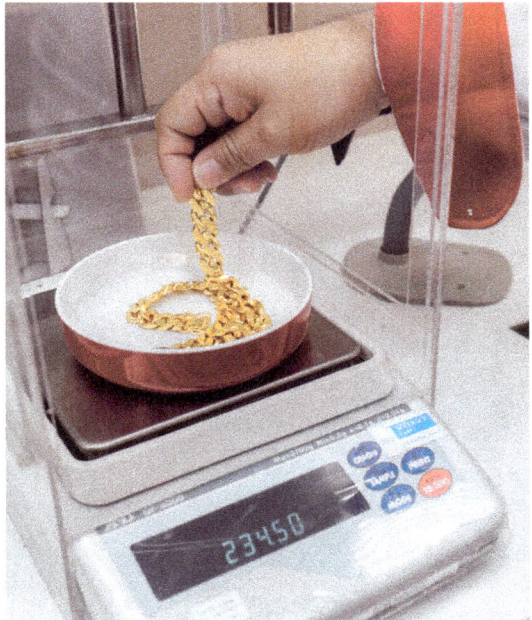

An Idiom to Describe Your Business?

历史悠旧，信誉卓越

*"Hard work, hard work and
more hard work.
One cannot but emphasise
this repeatedly..."*

Company Profile

Viking Offshore and Marine Limited is listed on the Singapore Exchange and based in Singapore with a presence in the Asian region and customers all over the world.

Through several wholly-owned subsidiaries, Viking provides offshore and marine system solutions to yards, vessel owners and oil majors around the world. Their competitive advantage lies in robust engineering designs, superior project delivery and a strong track record of delivering over the years.

Besides its offshore and marine services, Viking also moved into the mainstream offshore and marine, oil and gas industry sector by offering asset chartering services for oil and gas related assets.

Memorable Setbacks

Setbacks are never memorable but at the same time provide valuable lessons to be learnt and not repeated. In the earlier years of building the business, Viking had a failed investment after acquiring a business which had subsequently gone bad. Not only did they suffer financial losses, it was also a setback to their growth momentum and eroded confidence to a good extent.

The key thing is that they kept going, embarking on further acquisitions as part of a growth plan. Subsequent investments proved to be better executed and were an important strategy to growing the company. As the saying goes, "a ship will be safe in the harbour, but that's not what a ship is built for." Likewise, Viking realised they could shy away from acquisitions and growth and just focus on maintaining the current business, but that would be staying stagnant.

Learning Points

To say patience is a virtue might be over-stretching it, yet it is an important attribute for successful business growth. That is not to say we should be relaxed or have a lack of urgency and procrastinate. Viking was more than enthusiastic to quickly ramp up business, but also careful that certain aspects of the investment required more in-depth due diligence and analysis to ensure it was the right decision. While there is a saying that "we might miss the boat", Viking has learned over the years that there will be other boats that come along, and they might be better ones.

In contrast to patience, decisive action is also important. Once it was determined that the failed investment was not good, they were able to take decisive steps to mitigate and limit the damage. There is no time and avenue for sentimentality and the common saying of "cut your losses" is appropriate once such a conclusion is reached.

Advice to Budding Entrepreneurs

Hard work, hard work and more hard work. One cannot but emphasise this repeatedly. There's a lot of hard work, sacrifice, sweat, tears and anxiety that goes into building and managing businesses. To sum it up, it is about having the passion for it — you must crave the rewards that derives from success and embrace the heartache that comes with it. And if you are not prepared to bear with that, you would do better staying away from it — as the saying goes, get out of the kitchen if you cannot take the heat.

Get help — this is especially critical for budding entrepreneurs. Building a business is not a super man's job. The entrepreneur must recognise this and get help and get it early and at every stage of the business's development. It is important to build organisational capability and capacity in order for a business to be successful, viable and sustainable. Bring in the right professional managers at the appropriate juncture. Support of bankers and financiers are as important as adequate financial resources to a business's viability and growth.

Must-have Qualities of Successful Entrepreneurs

Passion for business is a key and all-embracing attribute for successful entrepreneurs. Unless you inherited a business, which you will still need to continue maintaining and growing, you will find that all entrepreneurs are driven individuals, passionate about business and to a certain extent fanatical about what they are doing. Mr Ong Choo Guan says he has not heard or known of anyone who is a reluctant entrepreneur. Passion gives you the energy to start, continue and cross the finish line. Passion gives you the encouragement to get up and fall over and over again until you achieve your goal. Passion gives you the interest to keep going, knowing that it is not enjoyable or sunny every day and in fact rainy most days with frequent thunderstorms.

Following on from passion is the undauntable willpower needed to succeed. Entrepreneurs must not be afraid to fail. Yes, they must detest failure but at the same time not be afraid of failure, and pick themselves up quickly from every failure to embark on the next challenge.

Lastly, a successful entrepreneur is someone who is biased for action. He/she must be a go-getter and not someone who will look left, look right, front and back and at the end of the day still not make the first move. This is almost akin to paralysis through analysis; whereby analysis after analysis is made and yet no action taken. Along the same line, he must be able to operate on less than perfect information and adapt and overcome challenges along the way; but still make the first step. To sum it

up, an individual who lives by the entrepreneurial mantra, is never bogged down with fear or uncertainty and never afraid of adapting when required.

Turning Point

During the early days, Viking's business diversification strategy to move upstream was crucial. Seeing the tough conditions of the system integration business evolving into a labour-intensive business with increasing competition and price pressures, they embarked onto asset ownership and chartering services. This move strengthened the balance sheet with hard assets and a more predictable, stable, sustainable and higher-margin income stream. They are already seeing early success and further expansion of the asset portfolio will give greater economic value.

Significant Milestones in Developing Your Business

In thinking of the three significant milestones, Mr Ong cannot help but quote the apt words of Sir Henry Ford — "Coming together is a beginning; keeping together is progress; working together is success."

The group is all about the coming together of various businesses which in the past were individual local companies operating on their own. Through a series of mergers and acquisitions, they were able to form a group of companies along the offshore and marine industry value chain. Following the formation of the group, the next challenge and milestone is the integration of the various businesses so that they are able to derive synergy and value enhancement where the whole is larger than the summation of its parts.

Last but not least, as discussed earlier, a key milestone and turning point to strengthen the business sees them venturing into the mainstream, by having an asset-based chartering services business. This will hopefully be the catalyst for Viking's next growth phase.

The Next 50 Years

This is a difficult topic for discussion without having a crystal ball to look into and predict what the future has in store. The industry will go through many cyclical ups and downs in the next 50 years. The business and organisation will continue to adapt and negotiate these cycles as they have done over the last 20 years. Viking will still focus their business growth, both horizontally and vertically, in the energy sector, and with more business facets added to the portfolio.

The oil and gas and the offshore and marine sectors will continue to exist. The emerging of new energy sources in terms of renewable energy may impact the industry to a certain extent, but by and large, the industry players will adapt and continue to shape the industry. For now, oil and gas will continue to be the mainstay of the global energy sources for supply and likewise, demand.

Major Contributions to the Economy

To say the business contributes majorly to the economy will be an overstatement, but in their little way, Viking does play a part in Singapore's economic growth.

For one, Viking supports customers who are major shipyards, who in turn are major contributors to the economy as Singapore is reputed as an offshore rig builder.

Headquartered in Singapore, Viking provides jobs for Singapore and consumes products and services from suppliers and service providers in Singapore.

Last but not least, as a listed group on the Singapore Exchange, it also contributes to the vibrancy of the capital markets.

Representing Singapore Internationally

While they may not be an internationally renowned brand, they can still be proud of the fact that all their businesses are homegrown, with close to 20 years of operating history. As they expanded overseas, customers from abroad will know of their home being in Singapore. In time, their continued track record of providing good solutions and services will represent Singapore well in the international offshore and marine industry arena.

Name a Local Dish that Best Represents You or Your Business.

The Chinese New Year favourite "Yu Sheng" comes to mind. It is an auspicious

delicacy served during every New Year. The various blessings and significance behind each ingredient that goes into the dish is also what Viking hopes to bring to the table. The lack of one ingredient will not complete the dish and this aptly describes Viking's various businesses coming together for the success of the group — 年年有余!

Giving Back

Without a doubt, businesses must carry the flag of corporate social responsibility. The community provides the necessary infrastructure for the business to operate conducively, their academic institutions churn out the skilled resources to hire into the business, and on and off, the community has to make way or bear with inconveniences from business operations. Morally, a case can be made for businesses to give back to society.

Company Culture

At every opportunity Viking encourages and fosters an environment and culture of teamwork and operational integration. This has and will continue to help in their business growth. As they are a group of companies of various businesses, only through operational integration and teamwork will they be able to achieve success through synergy, cross pollination of ideas and business opportunities, resources optimisation, congruent goal orientation and ease of doing business with customers. Customers no longer like to see a harmonised operation with a common touch point — they demand it.

Additionally, they are still considered a mid-sized setup and as such do not have the arrogance of big established operations and practice a mantra of striving for continuous operational excellence to win customers over.

Wanin Industries Pte Ltd

CEO Jerry TAN Tjin Hong

*"The business world is not a forgiving place.
It can tear you down, and as the saying goes,
only the strongest survive."*

Company Profile

Established in 1986 by a team of closely-knit family members, Wanin pioneered the bulk bottled water and cooler rental industry in Singapore. Originally commencing operations in Singapore, it has since started up its own factory in Johor in 1990, and expanded its marketing operations to Kuala Lumpur the following year. Pere Ocean is now going global, exporting to other parts of the World, i.e. Australia, China, Japan, Indonesia, Hong Kong and Sri Lanka, just to name a few.

Currently, Pere Ocean, a subsidiary of Wanin, is the only Singaporean-owned water company producing its own fresh natural mineral water from its own natural source, set in a green and clean environment. As providing quality water products and excellent service to its drinkers is the company's main priority, Pere Ocean is committed to excellence throughout every facet of its production process, logistics and customer services.

Memorable Setbacks

Back in the early 90s when the market was booming, the company contemplated entering the concrete wire mesh manufacturing industry. Having already placed a huge sum as deposit for the machinery, it was abruptly decided to forfeit the money and not proceed with the project, following on from the advice of elders. Not long after that, news came about of many defaulters in the market who could not make payment to suppliers. This goes to show that market research is important before entering the market. If we had done thorough market research earlier, we could have redirected the cashflow into a profit making project. Since then, we've taken a much more calculated and conservative approach to investing and growing the business.

Advice to Budding Entrepreneurs

Believe in yourself and your idea. This does not mean recklessness or being too risk-averse. Do your necessary research, understand the market, understand your product and understand the importance of timing. Starting a new business always involves a certain level of risk, yet try to mitigate unnecessary risks and take the leap. The first step is always the hardest but without it, there will be no journey.

Must-have Qualities of Successful Entrepreneurs

The business world is not a forgiving place. It can tear you down, and as the saying goes, only the strongest survives. These are three must-have qualities every successful entrepreneurs must have:

- Be courageous, because there will be days you will need to make difficult decisions that do not go down well with others, and there are days you will feel alone. It is this courage that will see you through.
- Have tenacity, the determination and perseverance to see the job through when others around you falter or give up. Maintain that fixity of purpose to outstand and outlast your competitors.
- Cultivate the ability to adapt. Be ready to adapt when the situation or environment calls for it. This skillset will make you more resilient in foreign environments.

Turning Point

In 1995, Wanin opted for a more aggressive strategy towards market expansion. That year, we bought into a competitor which then doubled our customer base. The move secured the company's position as the leading bottled water solution provider in Singapore for years to come.

The Next 50 Years

At Wanin Industries, we envision ourselves as "the preferred regional supplier for healthy beverage solutions". Through constant upgrading to the latest technologies and filtration methods, we make every effort to retain the essence of pure natural mineral water. The team has started planning for the future by recruiting like-minded talents and grooming them for a smooth transition into the new era while retaining Pere Ocean's core values.

In recent years, we have noticed a shift in the F&B industry. Consumers are getting health conscious and are educated to make a healthier choice in their eating habits. Shoppers pay more attention to the labels and ingredients used. If they believe a product is higher in quality and from a safe manufacturer, they will pay a premium for peace of mind. In the next 50 years, buying behaviour will lean towards companies that have established themselves as an ethical producer of healthy consumables.

Major Contributions to the Economy

Since the establishment of the company, Wanin Industries has been providing healthy, clean, natural spring water to daily users. For the health-conscious seeking an alternative to high calorie sweetened drinks, Pere Ocean Natural Mineral Water is the substitute. During several crises, water has proved essential to survival; from the tsunami in Aceh to the Fukushima blast in Japan and last year's Malaysian East

Coast flood, the company was one of the first in Singapore to respond with aid. During the passing of Mr. Lee Kuan Yew, as Singaporeans flocked in their droves to parliament house under the blistering heat, Pere Ocean Mineral Water bottles were on hand to quench the people's thirst. Bottled in a convenience pack, everyone is assured of refreshing mineral water readily available in most supermarkets and convenience stores.

Representing Singapore Internationally

Singapore has been known for being a clean, green environment and supplying only top quality products worldwide. Wanin is aiming high to represent Singapore by only producing the best quality products at an affordable price.

Major Influence and Inspiration

My father has been a great source of energy and major influence during his younger days. His words have been an inspiration to how to lead his business, life and family. He was a driven individual who set his sights high, and mentored others to achieve these goals together. He was strict but only because he wanted the best for everyone, from his staff to his family. This taught me to see the best in people and to cultivate a culture of learning within the organisation.

Name a Local Dish that Best Represents You or Your Business

A local dish or fruit that best represents the business would be a coconut. With its hardy shell, it survives through tough weather and grows on difficult grounds. This business is hardy and still experienced growth during the financial crisis. The coconut is also regarded as a source of life for the thirsty when resources are scarce. Similarly, when natural disasters occur, Wanin is able to contribute more to society by being an additional source of safe, clean drinking water.

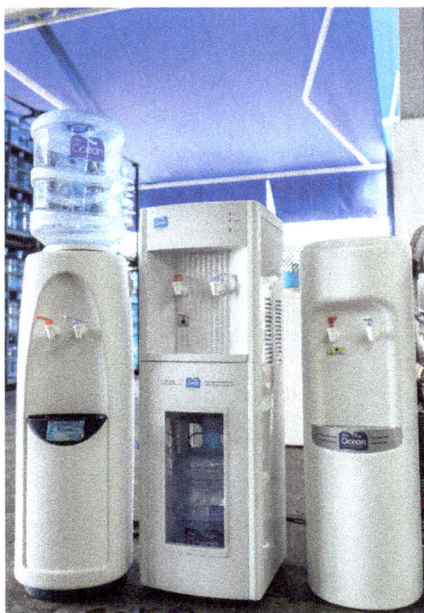

Company Culture

The company culture revolves around family values and encourages teamwork in the workplace. It is essential for everyone to work cohesively and communicate frequently as the business revolves around logistics. Coordination between the office, factory and delivery has to be timely to meet tight schedules. We build teamwork through annual retreats overseas, team-bonding activities such as BBQ sessions and bringing in trainers to familiarise new staff and refresh existing ones.

An Idiom to Describe Your Business

The idiom "饮水思源" best describes Wanin and its philosophy. In the literal sense, it means to show gratitude to the source of the water you are drinking from. It is also with this mentality that Wanin does business. Without the community and staff support we would not be where we are today. Therefore we must show gratitude by providing only the best for them. It was with this idea that the company's vision and mission was born: "The preferred regional supplier for healthy beverage solutions".

Business Philosophy

My business philosophy has been influenced by both my father and father-in-law, described in two chinese idioms.

My father: "处事待人，以和为贵", and my father-in-law: "害人之心不可有，防人之心不可无". We have to be harmonious in the way we work with all parties, whether they are our own family, staff, suppliers or customers. And while we aim for profit, we cannot do so unscrupulously and cause harm to others. However, we must always be wary and careful in the things we do when dealing with others so that we may provide a safe product for our customers, and a safe environment for our staff.

*"Change is the only constant,
and the needs of the world are ever-changing."*

Company Profile

XMH Holdings Ltd started as a small machinery repair and maintenance shop in Kitchener Road in 1955. With a history of over 50 years, the Group is now a reputable and trusted name as a diesel engine, propulsion and power generating solutions provider to a diverse customer base in the marine and industrial sectors across Asia. Over the years, the Group has expanded its primary product offerings to include reputable brands for which it has acquired distributorship, agency and dealership rights. The Group continued to advance, scaling up the value-chain with the introduction of "AceGen", its in-house range of power generating sets, and "XMH IPS", a one-stop integrated solution for vessel owners who require diesel engine (or electricity) driven propeller-based propulsion systems.

Moreover, XMH completed two acquisitions in recent years. The first is of Mech-Power Generator Pte Ltd ("MPG") in September 2013, a leading manufacturer of diesel powered generator sets and the second is Z-Power Automation Pte Ltd ("ZPA") in March 2015, a company which specialises in integrated marine automation products.

With the acquisitions, the Group's business activities can be broadly categorised into (i) distribution and provision of value-added products and services; (ii) after-sales services, trading and others; and (iii) assembly and installation of standby generator sets and provision of related services. The Group's marine products are marketed to shipyards, vessel owners and dealers whilst its industrial products are distributed to hotel proprietors, building owners and main contractors for a wide range of applications.

Setbacks and Recovery

It has to be the financial crisis in 1997. The market saw massive swings in exchange rates and interest rates, leading clients to withdraw their orders, causing a spike in the company's inventory. As clients stopped paying, XMH was struggling to meet the payment obligations to suppliers and banks. It was like the entire business operations and financial systems had stopped.

CEO Mr Tan Tin Yeow learnt a few profound lessons through this. Firstly, never give up; you have to be persistent and positive. There is no hardship that one cannot overcome, and one must always believe things will get better. Secondly, always work hard and be vigilant. Grasp the opportunities before others and swiftly capitalise on them. Lastly, always be prepared and have the risk management systems in place. Never assume that everything will remain constant and never underestimate any potential threats as it could very well unravel into huge problems.

Advice to Budding Entrepreneurs

There are no shortcuts to becoming a successful entrepreneur. An entrepreneur is commonly seen as an innovator and generator of new ideas and business processes. Being an entrepreneur and leader, you must be willing to take risks, exercise initiative, and take advantage of market opportunities by innovating new or improving existing products.

Must-Have Qualities of Successful Entrepreneurs

- Perseverance and Passion
- Effectiveness and Efficiency
- Vision

Turning Point

The quest to be global and the attainment of exclusive distributor rights from various principals, especially with Mitsubishi Heavy Industries Pte Ltd ("MHI"), formerly known as Mitsubishi Heavy Industries Engine System Asia Pte Ltd ("MHIESA"), for a range of Mitsubishi engines.

Through expansions, XMH also explored new revenue streams to increase market share and entered countries like Indonesia, Malaysia, Vietnam, China. These efforts led to the exclusive and non-exclusive distributorship rights of a wide product range of reputable brands in the region.

Since then, XMH Holdings Ltd continued to expand and became a publicly listed company. The listing has given us the opportunity to expand rapidly through acquisitions and joint ventures which have strengthened capabilities and our presence in the region.

Significant Milestones

It all started in the 1960s when our founder, Mr Tan Tum Beng started to buy used industrial diesel engines and machinery from suppliers in the United Kingdom through commissioned agents for resale. He would also modify such industrial diesel engines for customers in the timber industry. This was the beginning of a journey towards diversification to not only providing maintenance and repair services, but also the sale and modification of engines.

First Milestone

The first milestone in developing the business was when he saw the potential in used industrial and marine diesel engines and related machinery manufactured

in Japan. These were more competitively priced than those manufactured in the United Kingdom and they were gaining popularity in Singapore and Malaysia back then. In 1981, the business expanded to include the sale of used industrial and marine diesel engines and re-lated machinery from Japan. This expansion allowed the business to grow into one of the leading suppliers of used industrial and marine diesel engines and related machinery manufactured in Japan.

We continued to source and grow our quantity of purchases and range of products to suit the growing needs of clients. Staying relevant to market needs, we revised the business strategy to focus on securing distributorship, agency or dealership rights for new industrial and marine diesel engines, power generating sets and their respective genuine spare parts. Over the years, the Group has been recognised by MHI as the largest worldwide distributor for marine diesel engines for nine consecutive years since 2005.

Second Milestone

In the 2000s, the second milestone marked the continuation of XMH's tradition of innovation as we made our initial foray into the OEM business, developing and marketing a range of power generating sets under our in-house brand, "e-Gen", now renamed "AceGen". The "AceGen" power generating sets offer models with standardised features and models with customisable features to cater to the specifications of customers.

Third Milestone

The third milestone was XMH's listing on the SGX. The listing provided a platform for higher growth through capital funding for mergers and acquisitions. It helped to achieve rapid growth through acquisitions of companies that provided synergistic value such as Mech-Power Generator Pte Ltd ("MPG") and Z-Power Automation Pte Ltd ("ZPA"). It also allowed us to acquire a new building at Tuas Crescent, where we are able to house the business under one roof and give ourselves the ability to develop marinised engines in-house.

The Next 50 Years

No one can say they know for sure exactly what is going to happen 50 years down the road, so I hesitate to predict what the market environment will be like that far down.

However, as XMH has done over the last 60 years of its history, I anticipate that the company will continue to reinvent itself to stay relevant and successful. Through a culture of strong learning and collaboration, we have holistic staff growth and continuity of knowledge. We have a dedicated and experienced management team who have over 20 years of knowledge in the product and industry, business networking and management capabilities. It provides them with the ability to identify market trends and viable business opportunities, and stay ahead of the curve.

Already, we are looking at developing our own marinised engines in-house and further expanding our presence in Vietnam and Indonesia. This is a big step for XMH as it opens up our capabilities and streamlines costs.

Industry Trends in the Next 50 Years

The offshore and marine industry is not in the best position currently, but this is just part of a global cycle. Overall, the current downtrend is due to the uncertainty of oil prices and the slowing global economic growth. In the next 50 years, there will definitely be another slowdown or boom; upswings and downturns are inevitable.

At XMH, we have experienced our fair share of economic growth and decline, being in the industry for 60 years. What we can do is try to pre-empt and improve ourselves through identifying opportunities and capitalising on them. Looking to the future, we see a couple of trends that could represent key opportunities.

The trend of larger vessels means larger engines. The need for greener and more efficient engines coupled with increased regulations call for better quality engines, which we are no stranger to. Also, the developments in technology and its support requirements are leading to a rise in global need for data centres. Rampant growth of technological advances in this day and age calls for an increase in centres to store all the information. Data centres require power to cool the equipment and backup generators to maintain stable power should the power fail. Singapore in particular, with its key location and infrastructure, has been known to be a key country in the region to play a part as a home for data centres.

In addition to this, governments in the region, for example Indonesia and Vietnam, have announced initiatives to improve their infrastructure, to increase the defence of territorial waters and to enlarge their fishing fleets. These improvements will require engines and generators, be it in buildings or in ships. This could work in our favour and we can expect a steady influx of orders.

Major Contributions to the Economy

The business has contributed to the economy through global recognition, provision of products and services, and sparking innovation.

Through our strong performance, XMH has gained recognition from international brands. This attracts the attention of other brands to Singapore, especially if they are looking to Singapore as a hub to springboard themselves into the region.

The services and products XMH offer have given both local as well as international companies exposure to better quality engines and generators. This aids them in building a strong business and thus a stronger economy for us all.

We also continuously innovate. Therefore, with a culture of innovation, we feel we have pushed others to propel themselves to greater heights.

Representing Singapore Internationally

From a Singaporean startup back in the 1950s, XMH has come a long way to become the largest worldwide distributor for a globally recognised brand. We are known in the international community as a business that provides quality support, services and products. We have acquired distribution rights from many other well-known brands over the years as we prove our perseverance and dedication when an opportunity presents itself.

Singapore has enabled XMH to place itself on the world stage as we were contracted to support our world renowned airport, Changi Airport in building its Terminal 4 extension.

In the region, many clients know that XMH provides quality services and they always come back because they get products that are efficient and lasting, reflecting the "Singapore Standard".

Major Influence and Inspiration

A major influence and inspiration to me is my father. He was originally from Southern China. He neither went to school nor had any skills. While he lived a hard life in the early days, he endeavoured to improve the family's lives through hard work. He was a man of honesty and great trust, a fast learner with a unique acumen of the economy and of business related matters.

The company encountered a lot of difficulties in the early days. They could not secure sufficient financing from the banks or do business directly with overseas suppliers; they were not able to expand their client network quickly as they did not have a proper workshop and equipment; they faced a lot of challenges as they did not have the required skilled labour; they even suffered a fire that burnt down everything they had, causing them to have to start all over again. However, none of these obstacles set him back and only made him more resilient.

At first, I joined the company just to help my father out and to lessen his work load as he was getting older. Instead, he taught me everything in the business from scratch. It was through working with him that I was inspired to become a true entrepreneur.

My father and I are very close, we talk often and he is still an inspiration. From his insight and strong belief, I learnt to persevere and overcome many challenges in the business.

Name a Local Dish that Best Represents You or Your Business

I would have to say Nasi Lemak. On the surface, Nasi Lemak started as a relatively simple dish. Traditionally, Nasi Lemak is essentially made up of coconut rice, ikan bilis (anchovies) and sambal chilli. Because it is so simple, everything has to be on point, the rice has to be fragrant and of the right texture, the ikan bilis has to be fresh and crispy and most importantly the sambal chilli has to be perfect in consistency and flavour. Currently, many vendors have designed their Nasi Lemak to include an assortment of dishes that can accompany it, ranging from chicken wings to sambal prawns and many other choices.

Similarly, the business may seem simple on the surface. However, through the years we too have evolved and expanded our services and range of products. We now represent 20 major brands with over 4000 products across countries in the Asia-Pacific region.

Notwithstanding the above, we always ensure our true flavour is ever present, the fundamentals of excellent service, constant innovation and quality products.

Giving Back

I feel that everyone has a part to play in environmental safety and corporate and social responsibilities.

If the environment that you live in remains stagnant, there is a high chance you are going to remain stagnant too. If you promote innovation and kindness in your surroundings, I think it would be a more conducive environment for everyone to live and prosper.

I am very thankful for the environment around me, the people that have influenced and helped me and the company which has put its trust in me.

Company Culture

In XMH, we have a culture that inculcates strong learning and ethics, paired with great teamwork. This is essential to what we are today. We want to ensure innovation and experiences are passed on to all staff, creating the fundamentals of a strong business.

Change is the only constant, and the needs of the world are ever-changing. Identifying needs, learning new techniques and information, and staying competitive in the global environment helps the company stay relevant. When you pair innovation with ethics and complete tasks as one unified company, it results in high standards of accuracy and effectiveness, and a premium of ideas, which propels the business to the next level.

Having a culture of learning also allows us to have excellent business continuity; giving us the luxury of constant evolution and helping us to stay ahead.

An Idiom to Describe Your Business

A very simple idiom that you may have heard of, "the ball is in your court"; it basically means that it is your move to make. In life, there is always a smart move to make or the perfect angle to position yourself; it is just whether you grasp the opportunity and execute it within an acceptable timeframe. If your timing is poor, you are more likely to miss your target.

Zero Spot Laundry Service Pte Ltd

CEO Alex TEO H. M.

*"Zero Spot has showcased what a traditional
trade can achieve through automation
and productivity enhancement."*

Company Profile

Zero Spot was started in 1989 as a small laundry operator by co-founders Mr Lim Chin Hwee and Mdm Teo Siew Leng. Armed with a small investment of S$30,000 and a clutch of customers, the initial years were daunting as well as exciting. In seven years, with perseverance and unrelenting hard work, the company grew rapidly.

Today, Zero Spot has moved to a bigger plant to accommodate a bigger capacity. Yet it was as far back as 1997 when they invested in state-of-the-art equipment and technology to cope with the ever-rising business.

With the help of automation, Zero Spot has also diversified into the hotel and healthcare industries and landed a big contract to service Marina Bay Sands. To manage and sustain the growth, operations were professionalised and they started bringing in a middle management team and invested in them with an eye towards the future.

By staying true to their strong core values and vision, Zero Spot is now the leader in the industry and is starting to go regional.

Since then, they have embarked on a journey to become a leader in textile services and also provide textiles and technology solutions like RFID to many of their local and overseas partners.

Lessons Learnt

An ill-judged investment into a business they had little knowledge of brought the company into financial difficulties. Luckily, there was external help to tide them over the crisis.

Lessons learnt: be mindful of one's ability and judgement. Grow from strength to strength and do not over commit.

Must-have Qualities of An Entrepreneur

Your success factors shall one day become your failures. Always be prepared to learn, unlearn and relearn.

Significant Milestones

- Started automation early in the late 90's
- Built a team for the future
- Enterprise 50 Award

The Next 50 Years

Regional expansion as well as consolidation of their market leader position within Singapore are paramount. Zero Spot hopes to build on a solid foundation to ride the crest of Asia's growth. With better succession planning, they also expect to become the leader in the textile services industry, a new business vertical, in Asia.

The industry has existed since the day mankind started using textiles. However, expect more changes and innovation with technology moving at a very fast pace. One cannot see how the industry will develop in 50 years. It is definitely beyond our imagination.

Major Contributions to the Economy

The industry is closely related to hospitality and healthcare which have seen major developments in Singapore for the past 20 years. Being the largest operator in Singapore in terms of market share, this should be the first direct contribution. Zero Spot also benchmarks themselves in terms of remunerations and give more back to staff, a key success factor for the company. Lastly, they see themselves playing a more important role in the region in the next few years as the development in Asia gathers pace.

Representing Singapore Internationally

Zero Spot has shown what a traditional trade can achieve through automation and productivity enhancement. At the same time, their branding and achievements are an example to many countries. They are taking a leading role and contributing to development in some of these countries, thus proudly representing Singapore internationally.

Name a Local Dish that Best Represents You or Your Business

Roti-prata. Roti-prata needs to go through many flips, much like what the business has gone through for the past 26 years. Sometimes we even get ourselves into a hot plate, just like roti-prata. But when roti-prata is fried, the crispiness and fragrance makes it very tasty. With a good curry, which represents the management team, this will make the roti-prata complete.

Company Culture

Company culture is a very important factor in Zero Spot's growth and success. A strong, family-like culture, married with good management, is a great foundation for the future.

An Idiom to Describe Your Business

"A traditional trade that does not need to be managed in a traditional way."

KPMG

KPMG's Enterprise team offers valuable perspectives, ideas and options to help business owners and entrepreneurs capitalise on opportunities that drive business innovation and growth. Drawing on industry insight and technical knowledge, our professionals assist clients in their pursuit of business growth, enhanced performance, governance and compliance objectives.

In today's regulatory environment, our professionals can help companies navigate complex and fast-paced challenges at every stage of your journey. We can help you through every stage of your business lifecycle, from establishing your operations and raising capital, to international expansion, and complying with regulatory requirements. Our expertise include corporate tax, Mergers and Acquisitions, cyber security and information technology to help companies drive competitive advantage.

Business owners may consider seeking new perspectives from platforms such as the Enterprise 50 Awards jointly run by KPMG and the Business Times. The E50 Awards recognise outstanding performances by home-grown, privately-owned enterprises, and also provide a platform for those enterprises to self-assess and compare themselves with their peers.

Whether you are local or global, our professionals can help you gain access to the resources of KPMG through a single point of contact — an adviser to your company. It is a local touch with a global reach.

For more information on how we can help you, please visit: *kpmg.com.sg/enterprise*

Acknowledgements

Rebekah Lin & Cheryl Chong
Co-Founders, 50 For 50, a project by The Social Co.

For more information,
please visit the movement's website at:
http://50for50.sg

Or find out more on social media here:
@50for50sg #50for50sg

Photographer
Yew Jia Jun
SidexSide Pictures
https://www.facebook.com/sidexsidepictures/

Special thanks to Doreen Liu and Chua Hong Koon
for their continued support and encouragement
in producing this book.

Special thanks to Union Steel Holdings for their donation
to Make-A-Wish Foundation (Singapore)